Introducing Systems Design

Second Edition

Steve Skidmore

 **BLACKWELL**

The right of Steve Skidmore to be identified as author of this work has been asserted in accordance with the Copyright, Designs and Patents Act 1988.

First published 1989

First published in USA 1989

Second edition 1996

Second edition published in USA 1996

2   4   6   8   10   9   7   5   3   1

NCC Blackwell
108 Cowley Road
Oxford OX4 1JF
UK

Blackwell Publishers Inc.
238 Main Street
Cambridge, Massachusetts 02142
USA

British Library Cataloguing in Publication Data
A CIP catalogue record for this book is available from the British Library.

Library of Congress Cataloging-in-Publication Data
Skidmore, Steve.
Introducing systems design/Steve Skidmore.
Cambridge, Mass. : NCC Blackwell, 1996.
p.   cm.
QA76.9.S88   S59   1996
005.1/2 20
1855542471 (pbk. : alk. paper)
Includes index.
Systems design.
95047493

ISBN 1 85554 247 1

Typeset in 10 on 12pt Caledonia and Frutiger
Printed in Great Britain by Hartnolls Ltd, Bodmin, Cornwall

This book is printed on acid-free paper

Contents

Preface

This book is the second of two texts about the development of computer systems. It presents a series of models and skills that should help the definition and delivery of high-quality information systems. This book is primarily concerned with logical and physical design.

The book is primarily aimed at:

- undergraduate and Higher National Diploma and Certificate students undertaking a module in systems analysis and design;
- students undertaking professional examinations;
- trainee analysts studying for professional qualifications or following professional development schemes;
- practising systems designers and developers.

Analysis and Design are two words in common currency in systems development. The preface to the companion text makes the point that the distinction is arbitrary and that analysis, design and development is used interchangeably throughout the text to provide some variety. However, it is worth highlighting how the content and split of the two books has been determined.

Introducing Systems Analysis is primarily about analysing business benefits and procedures. The Data Flow Diagram is introduced as a technique for modelling understanding of current systems and developing an overall functional architecture for fulfilling agreed requirements. Data Flow Diagrams are not well suited to design but they are an effective analysis model. The Logical Data Structure is also an effective architectural model, expressing the structure and size of systems more effectively than text. In our company we construct these models as part of our estimating process. The inclusion of Entity Life Histories in an analysis text is probably more controversial. However, we find that they do highlight facets of the system not illuminated by the other two models. Furthermore, they provide an introduction to an object perspective as well as a basis for later detailed design.

The content of the two books is also determined by what we feel comfortable in presenting in two one-week courses to practitioners. The material of both books can be comfortably covered in around 35–40 hours of study. Delegates usually take a break between the two courses to allow some time for reflection and relaxation! This duration also fits in (supported by exercises and assignments) with what inexperienced developers can accomplish in an academic term, semester or year depending upon the number of hours per week allocated to lecturers and tutorials.

I hope readers find this a practical introduction. In our own company (the 'we' of the text) I sit with other developers using, extending and selecting the tools and techniques covered here. This experience has forged the way I look at things and I would like to acknowledge their contribution. I have also spent a considerable amount of time explaining and exploring these models with users (in our software development projects) and delegates (on our training courses). Many have suggested changes and clarifications to the models, some of which have found their way into the two books in this series.

Finally, I would like to specifically acknowledge the following people who have helped my understanding of systems development and its teaching – Mike Crawford, Brenda Wroe, Gillian Mills, Andrew Parkin, David Helmy, David Howe, Ray Farmer, Frank Land and Ron Stamper.

Steve Skidmore

1 Context

1.1 Introduction

This book is concerned with models and techniques that translate the architectural model of analysis into a detailed design and implementation of an effective computer-based system.

In the context of the Systems Development Life Cycle (see figure 1.1 for our version) design consists of Logical Systems Design – expressing the design in a set of detailed models, and Physical Systems Design, which is concerned with the physical implementation of the logical models. Practical tasks and strategies for systems delivery and implementation are also covered in this book.

The Life Cycle and chapter structure (figure 1.2) may suggest that systems development is a linear process, achieved by simply progressing through the suggested stages without reflection or reassessment of what has been previously considered and decided. This reflects teaching necessity rather than practical experience. Design is an iterative activity and so readers are strongly urged to continually review their understanding of previous tasks so that they can strengthen their understanding of the whole design process.

There are many candidate design models. This text selects and presents a range of tools and techniques from an extensive toolkit in preference to describing

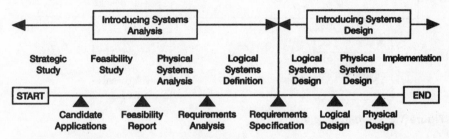

Figure 1.1 Systems development life cycle.

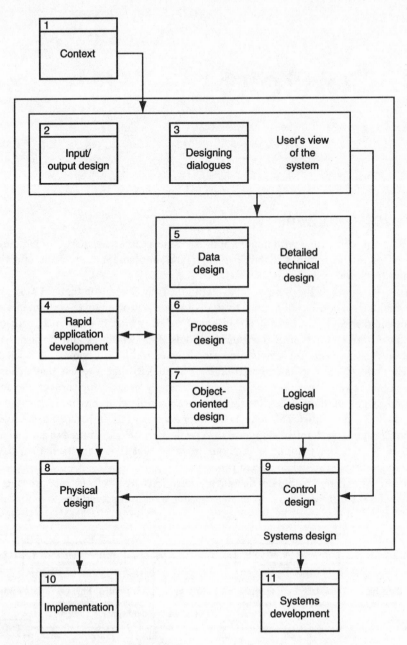

Figure 1.2 A road map of the text.

a prescriptive methodology. Several proprietary methodologies are available that aim to provide a packaged, structured set of techniques and guidelines for their application within an organization – SSADM is a typical example. In contrast this book selects techniques from a number of sources and on occasions presents alternate models so their usefulness in different circumstances can be assessed by the reader.

1.2 Structure of the book

This chapter suggests objectives and constraints of design and briefly reviews the models introduced in the companion text *Introducing Systems Analysis*. It also looks at Computer Aided Software Engineering (CASE) and the impact it has had on systems development.

Chapter 2 looks at the inputs and outputs of the system. In most cases these are why application systems are built in the first place. The very reason for the existence of the system is to allow inputs (meter readings, orders, deliveries) to produce outputs (bills, invoices and roadsheets). Data collection must be accurate, minimal and easy. Outputs should be correct, informative and simple to understand. Input and output design is a subjective, practical aspect of the whole design task. It may not be as technically exciting as data or process definition but it is crucial.

Once inputs and outputs have been agreed, the developer needs to define the computer procedures to capture data and display and print output. These are the tasks of human–computer interface design and the subject of chapter 3. It examines the meaning of 'user friendly' and the ways that the dialogue can be structured in the system. The chapter concludes with a review of three dialogue models.

Chapter 4 looks at Rapid Application Development (RAD). This is based around four key elements:

- Prototyping;
- Computer Aided Software Engineering (CASE);
- Joint Application Development (JAD);
- Skilled small team development.

The advantages and disadvantages of prototyping are explored and applications and areas that might benefit from RAD are suggested.

Chapter 5 is concerned with logical data design based on the principles of Relational Data Analysis (RDA). It shows how a table structure can be developed from applying a set of standard rules to representative inputs and outputs. These tables are then converted into a Logical Data Structure (LDS) to give a graphical view of the data structures of the system.

The accurate and unambiguous specification of processes is at the heart of systems design. Chapter 6 presents two alternative methods of process specification – the Action Diagram and the Update Process Model. Readers are invited to compare the two against certain criteria to see which they feel is 'best' for a given set of circumstances. Two enquiry (or read only) process models are also shown to represent this area of systems design.

The Entity Life History produced in chapter 6 provides a good introduction to some of the principles of object-oriented development explored in chapter 7. Basic principles of this approach are explained and models introduced earlier in the text are explored within this new context. State charts are explained and comprehensive references given to further relevant reading.

Chapters 5, 6 and 7 are primarily concerned with logical systems specification. Chapter 8 gives a general review of the main issues that arise in moving from a logical to a physical data and program design.

Chapter 9 reviews legislative, software and clerical controls required in systems development. Details and implications of the Data Protection Act and the Computer Misuse Act are highlighted as well as the role of the Data Dictionary in recording and perhaps enforcing value, format and other software checks.

The practical tasks and strategies of implementation are covered in chapter 10 and finally, chapter 11 briefly reviews the objectives of systems design in the light of the models and methods developed in this book.

1.3 Objectives of design

Design builds on the objectives set for the information system in the Feasibility Report (see chapters 2 and 3 of *Introducing Systems Analysis*). However, the achievement of immediate business or enterprise objectives is only part of the story. There must also be a place for the overall elements of good design that are relevant across all applications.

The following list gives an indication of some of the desirable features of a 'good quality' design:

■ **Functional**. The system must support successfully the user's requirements. Design models should continue to refine our understanding of the system with the aim of minimizing misunderstandings. Mistakes are easier and cheaper to correct in models than in programs.
■ **Efficient**. This is concerned with meeting the functional requirements within the agreed time. There are three facets to this objective:
    – throughput: the ability to handle a specified number of documents per hour or day;
    – response time: to be able to respond to a request for information within a given time limit;
    – run time: the ability to undertake a whole processing task within a given time limit.
  Efficiency should also be extended to effective use of staff resources. For many organizations the cost of Information Systems (IS) staff is the most significant portion of their expenditure in this area. These employees must be used effectively and deliver value for money.
■ **Flexible**. Organizations are dynamic. They are affected by internal growth and politics, staff resignations and appointments, administrative reviews and re-organizations, external take-overs, policies and pressures, variations in customer preference and behaviour, economic recessions and political dogma. Consequently, information systems must be easy to adapt to new and changing requirements.

- **Portable**. Portability is closely linked to independence. The rate of technological change means that investment in existing systems will only be preserved if the designer takes effective measures to ensure that little conversion work is required to transfer a system from one computing environment to another. Systems built in this way can harness technical advances rather than reject them on the grounds of the 'cost of the re-write'.
- **Secure**. Data is a costly and hence valuable resource and so any system that collects and processes it must be resistant to breaches of privacy and confidentiality. Systems must also be designed to meet legislative requirements imposed by the Data Protection Act and the Computer Misuse Act.
- **Reliable**. Integrity is a further feature of good design. Parkin describes good integrity when 'all the desired data is accurately recorded, without omission, and stored on the computer safely, so that it is not accidentally or deliberately corrupted or lost'. Thus a system must be trustworthy and accurate and it must be able to demonstrate these qualities to internal and external auditors who have responsibility for checking the validity of the system.
- **Economical**. The need for a design that demands minimum storage for data and programs is probably a feature that has become less important as hardware costs have declined. Nevertheless, minimizing the amount of redundant data stored by the system reduces problems associated with amendment, insertion and deletion of data.
- **Usable**. A design may be assessed in terms of the ease with which it may be learned and operated within acceptable levels of human discomfort, tiredness, effort, etc. It has been suggested (Shackel, 1986) that the design process must be:
  – user-centred;
  – participative;
  – experimental;
  – iterative;
  – user-supportive.
  A usable system may be defined as one that is not only user friendly but also feels normal to use (Schott and Olson, 1988).
- **Maintainable**. The dynamic nature of business means that requirements must inevitably change over time. It must be easy to make these changes and the effect of implementing these changes must be understood. Good designs are simple and modular, so that the effect of change is both minimized and predictable. Maintenance is also made easier by the availability of accurate and complete documentation.

1.4 Constraints on design

The following list gives some idea of the possible constraints on design:

- **Budget**. The total system cost of meeting the functional requirements must be considered in the light of the available budget. 'Better' design – functionality, flexibility, portability, etc. often incurs greater expense and leads to costs outweighing benefits, hence making the project financially infeasible.

■ **Time**. The users of systems usually have two questions – how much will it cost and when will it be completed? Good design may delay system delivery. It will take considerable time to design, build and test adaptable interfaces that will enable the skill level of the user to evolve. This better design may produce long-term productivity but its development cost and time may rule it out completely.

■ **Resources**. Business and legal constraints may demand that a system has to be produced by a certain time. This means that a certain number and type of resources have to be available to complete the project If these resources are not available, but the time deadline is retained, then something has to give.

■ **Integration with other systems**. Existing and planned systems may limit the options and features available. System development rarely takes place in a 'greenfield' site where there is no previous system to exert its influence and impose constraints. In nearly all cases the designer must interface with existing hardware, use available software tools and collect data from other systems.

■ **Skills**. Limitations may arise from the range of skills and level of competence in both the design team and the planned users and operators of the system. Thus the design may reflect current strengths and practices of the information systems department (using COBOL on a mainframe, for example) rather than use methods and software that require skills that are known to be scarce in the market-place.

■ **Standards**. Internal standards may drive the design team in a particular direction, for example:
  ■ the hardware must be IBM;
  ■ COBOL must be used for software development;
  ■ ORACLE must be used for all database development.

Such objectives and constraints are normally defined in the requirements specification. Usability is a more difficult objective to consider. The following has been suggested (Schott and Olson, 1988):

  ■ the time taken to learn a system's basic concepts and master its operation;
  ■ the rate of occurrence and ability to recover from errors of a specific type;
  ■ the 'warm-up' time to re-learn after absence of the user;
  ■ attitudes (user satisfaction).

We would hope that the models and techniques introduced in this book would help us achieve objectives and control constraints. Consequently we will be re-visiting this list in the final chapter of the book.

1.5 The products of analysis

The models introduced in *Introducing Systems Analysis* offer three complementary perspectives of the system – data, process and event.

1.5.1 Logical data model: the data perspective

The Logical Data Model was constructed from a 'top-down' perspective, identifying entities and relationships before adding significant attributes. An informal approach to normalization was suggested and organizing the attributes led to the discovery of new entities and relationships. The data model is re-visited in this book, this time from a 'bottom-up' perspective based on the agreed inputs and outputs of the system. In practice the data model is a mixture of the two approaches, changing as more is understood about the data. It is a dynamic model that is first constructed from a partial 'top-down' analysis of the problem situation progressing into more definite form as the requirements become specified and agreed. We also find that delegates become better 'top-down' modellers after they have had the opportunity to experiment with 'bottom-up' rule following normalization. The relationships (which can look a bit haphazard from the top-down approach) are defined automatically in the bottom-up method. We have also found that practitioners familiar with data modelling have less difficulty in moving into object-oriented state design.

The Logical Data Structure (LDS) of figure 1.3 contains the main features of the diagram. Entities are things that the enterprise recognizes in the area under investigation and wishes to collect and store data about. Entities might be physical, conceptual or active and are expressed as a singular noun within a 'soft-box'. Entities are described by attributes (data items, elements). The value of one or more of these attributes (the identifier) uniquely identifies a particular entity occurrence. For example, order-number identifies one particular order. Relationships are relevant

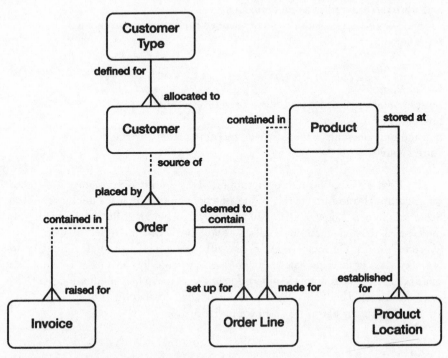

Figure 1.3　Logical data structure.

business connections between two entities. A relationship is represented on an LDS by a line linking the associated entities. Relationships are often of the degree one to many (1:m). For example, a Customer places many Orders, but each Order can only be placed by one Customer. In this instance there is a one-to-many relationship between Customer and Order, the many end of a relationship being represented by the crow's foot symbol on the end of the relationship line.

Relationships may also be 1:1. For example, an Order might lead to one Despatch Note and one Despatch Note may be for only one order. In certain methodologies 1:1 relationships are not permitted. It is usually suggested that the two entities are merged and that one of the identifiers is selected to identify the merged set. However, there are dangers in merging entities that do not have the same identifier (as in this example) and so a correct representation of the business rules shown by a 1:1 relationship is to be encouraged.

Many-to-many relationships are normally decomposed into two 1:m relationships with the addition of a link entity (see figure 1.4). In this example, the many to many relationship between Order and Product is resolved by the definition of the intermediate entity Order Line. It is here that we would record order-qty (the amount ordered of that Product on this Order).

A relationship is mandatory if an entity occurrence cannot exist without taking part in the relationship. For example an Order must come from a Customer. If this is not true then the relationship is optional – for example, a Customer need not have placed an Order. An unbroken line is used to show a mandatory relationship and a broken line to signify an optional one.

SSADM version 4 also introduced standardized relationship naming, following the convention:

each
Entity Name
must be/may be (shown by a broken or unbroken line)
link phrase
one and only one/one or more (shown by presence or absence of a crow's foot)
Entity Name

The Logical Data Structure is supported by entity descriptions and other information. The addition of this supporting documentation turns the Logical Data Structure into a Logical Data Model (LDM). The identifier of the entity is underlined or presented in boldface. Sometimes the identifier of one entity (Customer-no for Customer) appears in another data set (for example, Order) as an ordinary data item. This can be marked as a foreign key in Order by using an asterisk. This mark is not used where foreign keys make up the identifier (such as in Order Line). This convention is re-introduced in chapter 5 of this text. The attribute listing for figure 1.3 is shown in figure 1.5.

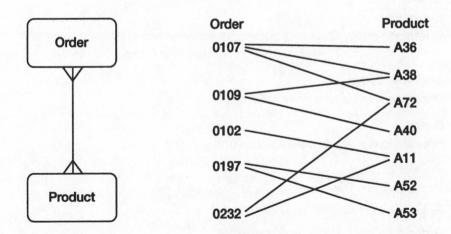

This shows that order 107 was for three products (A36, A38 and A72) and that A38 was also ordered on order no 0109 and A72 on order no 0232.

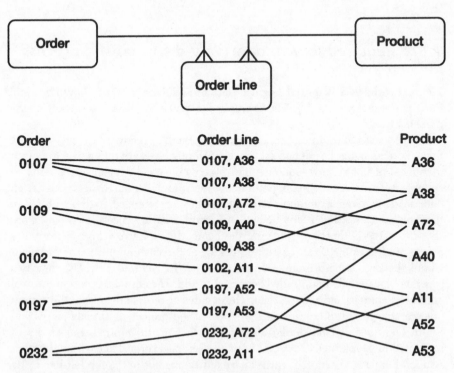

Figure 1.4 The decomposition of a many-to-many relationship.

Customer
Customer-code, Customer-name, Customer-address, *Customer-type,
Customer-credit-line, Customer-tel-no

Customer Type
Customer-type, Customer-credit-limit

Product
Product-code, Product-decription, Product-price

Product Location
Product-code, Bin-location, Amount-stored-in-bin

Order
Order-no, Order-date, *Customer-code

Invoice
Invoice-no, Invoice-date, *Order-no

Order Line
Order-no, Product-code, Order-qty

Figure 1.5   Attribute listing for the entities of figure 1.3.

1.5.2 Required logical data flow diagram: the process perspective

Figure 1.6 shows a Required Logical Data Flow Diagram (Data Flow Diagram) for a particular application. The example illustrates the basic constructs of the model.

Processes are transformations, changing incoming data flows into outgoing data flows. A rectangular box denotes a process. All processes are numbered to permit identification not to show sequence. The process is named with an active verb and an object or object clause. Open-ended rectangles denote data stores. Each data store is given a unique name and is cross-referenced to the entities of the Logical Data Model (see below). An arrow from a process to a data store shows a WRITE function (changing the data) while an arrow from a store to a process indicates a READ operation (looking at the data only). In circumstances where the data is both examined and changed (READ and WRITE) then two separate flows or a double-headed flow can be used. The ellipses represent external entities or sources and sinks of data. These enter or receive data from the system but are considered to be outside the scope of the project. Both data stores and external entities can be duplicated on the diagram to improve the clarity of presentation. Duplicated data stores have an additional vertical line within the store symbol. Duplicated external entities have a diagonal line at the top left-hand side of the ellipse symbol.

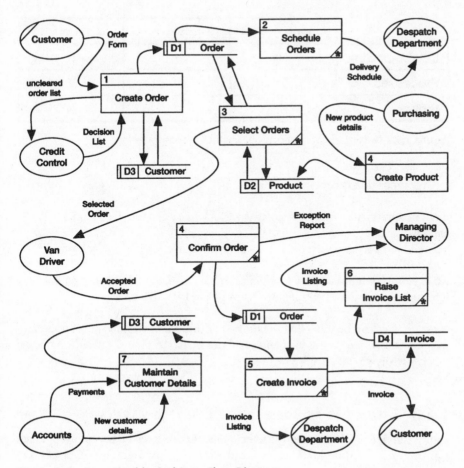

Figure 1.6 A required logical Data Flow Diagram.

Data flows are shown as simple arrowed lines connecting the external entities, processes and stores. Each line is given a simple, unique meaningful name. Data flows moving in and out of stores do not necessarily require names because the store name may be sufficient to describe the flow. However, in some instances it may be useful to use a name where the flow is especially significant or is not easy to discern from an examination of the diagram. The permitted connection of the elements of the Data Flow Diagram is shown in figure 1.7.

The Data Flow Diagram has a simple and consistent way of representing the successive modelling levels required in a hierarchy. Each process is exploded into a lower level Data Flow Diagram until the process can be written on Elementary Process Description in a Data Dictionary. In this way it is possible to present a series of Data Flow Diagrams representing increasing detail. Indeed the concept can be extended backwards to a one-process Context Diagram summarizing the inputs and outputs of the system under consideration.

	Source or Sink	Processes	Stores
Source or Sink	N	Y	N
Processes	Y	Y	Y
Stores	N	Y	N

Figure 1.7 Permitted connections between DFD components.

Decomposition is complete when:

Each process can be described in an A4 Elementary Process Description
and
There is no process with a read/write flow to a store
and
An exploratory interface line (showing the human–computer boundary) does not intersect any processes on the lowest level Data Flow Diagram.

Most systems can be modelled within two or three levels. The control of decomposition is examined again in chapter 6 of this book. An example of a decomposed process is shown in figure 1.8.

1.5.3 Entity life histories: the event perspective

Entity Life Histories consider the events that change stored data. An event is not a process, it is the stimulus that causes a process to be invoked. Three type of event can be distinguished:

- **External event**. A transaction arriving from the outside world. These are normally associated with data flows from external entities on the Data Flow Diagram.
- **Internal event**. This occurs when a predefined condition in the data has been met. For example, Stock level = Re-order level.
- **Time-based event**. These events take place at a given time or time interval.

The *effect* of each event on each entity is shown on an Entity/Event grid (see figure 1.9). The effect may be the:

Creation (C) of an entity occurrence
Deletion (D) of an entity occurrence
Modification (M) of data items in the entity occurrence. Modification is also said to take place when data items in created entity occurrences are inserted for the first time.

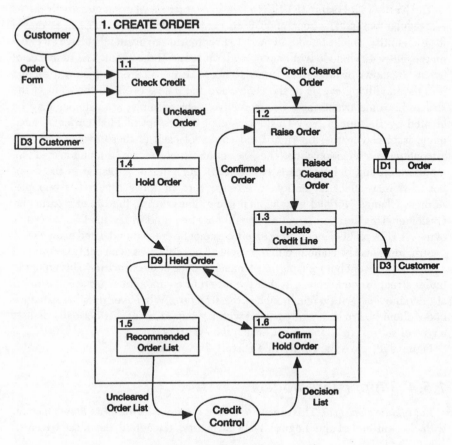

Figure 1.8 Level-2 DFD for process 1 of figure 1.7.

Event	Entity Customer
Receipt of new customer detail	C
Receipt of first order	C
Address change notified	M
Resignation received	D

Figure 1.9 Part of an entity/event grid.

The Entity Life History (ELH) is a tree-like structure where nodes are drawn as rectangular boxes. The root node is the entity and a separate ELH is drawn for each entity. The leaf nodes of the ELH represent the events that have an effect on the entity. Each node is annotated with the name of the event. The sequence of events is shown from left to right. Hence, the create event is shown on the left, the modifying events in the centre and the delete event to the right of the structure. Some events may be alternatives. For example, a Customer may be created by Receipt of New Customer detail *or* Receipt of First Order. A small circle is placed in the top right-hand corner of each of these events and both are put under a selection node. These selection structures can be found in creation, modification and deletion parts of the ELH. An asterisk is placed in the event box if it may affect an entity occurrence zero or more times. For example; Address Change Notified may happen many times during the life of a particular Customer. This iteration structure should only be found in the modification parts of the ELH. A particular entity occurrence cannot be created or deleted many times!

Structures may be combined to represent all possible lives of an entity occurrence as long as the event box remains the elementary node of the structure. This grouping under structure nodes ensures that the different component types are not mixed at the same level within one branch of the structure. Whenever possible structure nodes should be meaningfully named with a group heading that normally defines a type of sub-life or timeframe in which the events occur.

Figure 1.10 gives the Entity Life History for Customer.

1.5.4 Supporting models

Entity/data store grid. This cross-references the stores of the Data Flow Diagram with the entities of the Logical Data Structure. Except in the most trivial of

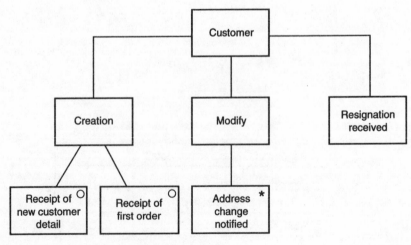

Figure 1.10 Entity life history for customer.

applications it is impossible to show every entity as a data store on the DFD. Consequently it is necessary to introduce a shorthand whereby one or more entities are grouped together into one data store. This grouping is solely for the purpose of retaining the clarity of the Data Flow Diagram and there is no suggestion that these are possible physical files defined later in the development process.

1.5.5 Data dictionary

The Data Dictionary holds the corporate data resource and provides a detailed underpinning of the other models described above. It records data about data elements, data structures, data flows, data stores and processes. The dictionary can be maintained on paper and manually compiled and updated. However, it is usual to hold the data on a DDS (Data Dictionary Software) package or in a CASE tool. Most cheap CASE tools (see later) offer this facility and hence it is difficult to envisage any situation where manual compilation will remain.

Introducing Systems Analysis also stated the need for good interpersonal skills to support the developer's technical abilities. This remains true in systems design and two eminent authors have emphasized its importance within the debate about object-oriented development. Software engineering, they suggest, 'conjures up images of formulas, algorithms and 'hard scientific approaches', yet it is a very people-oriented business. When one of the authors asked how many educators in the audience required some interpersonal communications training as part of their software engineering program – *'no hands were raised.* Yet effective communication . . . is vital to successful systems analysis' (Coad and Yourdon, 1991).

1.6 CASE tools

Introducing Systems Analysis stressed the need for logical information systems models that are independent of organizational arrangements and hardware and software implementation. The same theme continues in this text. However, the adoption of such logical models extends the development life cycle. This increase in the number of activities has meant that the automation of some of these tasks is essential, otherwise the long development times associated with the life cycle become even greater. Ed Yourdon identified this perception of increased duration as one of the reasons organizations gave for not adopting a structured approach to systems development (Yourdon, 1986). Unfortunately the first generation CASE tools that supported the structured methods were usually cumbersome to use, had poor graphics and were too expensive (minimum £5,000 per workstation) for most development teams. Consequently, many organizations attempted to implement structured methods using manually constructed and maintained diagrams and dictionaries. This was a nightmare. Structured methods began to become synonymous with mounds of paper, meetings and bureaucracy.

In some organizations, CASE was introduced without any complementary investment in training staff in the modelling techniques or in effective project management. CASE automates the logical models. If you cannot model logically you cannot use CASE effectively. It is extremely difficult to 'pick-up' the model methods and purpose from experimenting with a CASE tool – it can be likened to trying to learn maths from a spreadsheet. Consequently, many of these organizations abandoned CASE as an expensive error and returned to their manual methods.

However, quality CASE tools are now available at a reasonable cost (£500 per workstation). These offer:

- **Diagramming of common models**. Diagrams can be constructed and edited. This produces high-quality documentation that is compliant with agreed standards. Changes can be made quickly and models re-printed.
- **Model verification against a Data Dictionary**. For example, the tool may highlight that a data item contained in an output does not enter the relevant process from an incoming data flow or store and is not produced by the process itself. The Data Dictionary information required to undertake such checks is maintained in the CASE tool and is, in my opinion, alone worth the price of the software.
- **The validation of models against each other**. This highlights inconsistencies between different views of the data. Many CASE tools define data stores from entities and so automatically produce the equivalent of our manual entity/data store grid.

CASE tools that offer these facilities are cheap and easy to cost justify. They provide productivity gains as well as producing high-quality documentation that gives a professional finish to our work. They are also cheap enough to be abandoned when better products become available.

In the division suggested by Slusky and re-printed from the first edition of this book (see figure 1.11; Slusky, 1987) this is a first-level tool. More sophisticated (and expensive) CASE tools are available that support the first-level features but also include prototyping facilities. In such tools logical screens can be developed for each incoming and outgoing data flow on the Data Flow Diagram. These screens allow the physical placement of the data items defined in the Data Dictionary and so permit the definition of logical order entry as well as the aesthetic layout of the screen. These logical screens can be linked through logical dialogues (menus, etc.) and the working of the system simulated for the user. Once this design is agreed many of these tools support automatic generation of the physical screen. Slusky also includes in this second set vendor specific tools that typically use Logical Data Models to drive physical database definition in the target RDBMS.

Slusky's third-level tools encompass the first two levels but introduce project management facilities for planning, control and execution of the project. Code generation is an important feature of these tools. Changes in requirements are integrated by changing the model(s) and re-generating the code, not by changing the code itself. In this way code and models are kept consistent (see chapter 4). We might also include at this level meta-CASE tools, software for constructing CASE tools. These allow diagramming notation, rules, constraints and semantics to be defined for a CASE tool to support a published standard or tailored methodology.

| CASE facilities | CASE categories | | |
| | Development | | Integrated control |
	Modelling CASE I	Prototyping CASE II	CASE III
Primary facilities			
Graphics	Yes		Yes
Data dictionary			
Environment entities	Yes	Yes	Yes
Application entities	Yes	Yes	Yes
Documentation			
Document graph	Yes		Yes
Word processing	Yes		Yes
Analysis			
Graphics analysis	Yes		Yes
Entities analysis	Yes	Yes	Yes
User input/output prototype			
Screen design	Yes	Yes	Yes
Data entry execution		Yes	Yes
Report design	Yes	Yes	Yes
Report execution		Yes	Yes
Data manipulation prototype			
Program generation		Yes	Yes
Program execution		Yes	Yes
Syntax conversion		Yes	Yes
Database prototype			
Database generation		Yes	Yes
Database query/update		Yes	Yes
System project management			
Project planning			Yes
Project execution			Yes
Project control			Yes
Auxiliary facilities			
Migration (export/import)			
Dictionary migration	Yes	Yes	Yes
Program migration		Yes	Yes
Database migration		Yes	Yes
Help maintenance	Yes	Yes	Yes
Custom modifications customisation for new methods and standards	Yes		Yes
Housekeeping			
Backup/restore		Yes	Yes
CASE set-up/monitoring		Yes	Yes

Source: Slusky, 1988

Figure 1.11 Summary of CASE tool facilities.

John Windsor has suggested the following effects of the implementation of CASE tools (Windsor, 1986):

■ CASE will provide the structure of the task. The software will demand a certain level of problem definition. If this is incomplete then development cannot continue. Documentation and project management standards play a similar role in manual development but are often foiled by the sheer complexity and diversity of the task. 'Flexible' humans permit incomplete definition on the grounds of achieving project deadlines.

■ CASE will permit the proper consideration of alternative designs. Currently, a developer only has time to pursue one basic design. Most other possibilities are discounted at an early stage because time and cost does not allow their proper evaluation. CASE tools permit the exploration of different boundaries, technologies and requirements by simulating the effect of these parameters: 'Through the use of the ability to quickly and easily investigate alternatives the analyst becomes capable of generating a "best" system, a system that will most closely meet the needs of the client' (Windsor, 1986).

■ Error handling, audit and security – usually addressed at the end of the development cycle – can be tackled much earlier in the project. Consequently, such factors become more integrated into the design, rather than tacked on at the end.

■ Delivered systems should be much more comprehensive and accurate. They should have a longer survival time because of the rigour of the development process.

■ The use of code generators should significantly speed up the coding part of the development life cycle. This also means that less time will be spent in unit and system testing (see chapter 10).

■ CASE software imposes and maintains documentation standards. This should make subsequent changes easier and their effects more predictable.

However, Windsor also feels that the major advantages of automated tools are also potential weaknesses. For example:

■ Standards may become too inflexible. The standards are driven by the tool rather than the needs of the organization, project or application area.

■ There are no rules to tell you when to stop investigating alternative systems.

■ Code generators may produce verbose programs that are slow to run and difficult to interface with other parts of the system.

1.7 Summary

This chapter has introduced the structure of the book and given examples of the models that should have been produced in Systems Analysis. The objectives and constraints of design have been presented and these will be examined again in chapter 11.

Finally, CASE (Computer Aided Software Engineering) has been explored and suggestions made about its impact on systems development. There is no doubt in my mind that the adoption of structured methods was held back by the high cost and low functionality of early CASE tools. This error is not being repeated by the object-oriented vendors. It was noticeable at a recent conference and exhibition that all the object methodologies were demonstrating and selling CASE tools – not plastic templates!

2 Input and Output Design

2.1 Introduction

The main objective of an information system is to produce data to support the operations and decision making of the enterprise. These will be the *outputs* of the system. Many of these outputs will be based upon information entered into the system. Information provided by employees, customers and other sources of *input*.

Much of this book is about structuring and processing data. However, it must always be recalled that the reason for the system in the first place is its outputs and inputs. Hence, effective design of both these areas is essential. Outputs should be clear, timely and relevant. Inputs should be minimal, accurate and easy to enter.

2.2 The design boundary

The starting point for input and output design is a set of levelled required Logical Data Flow Diagrams. These represent what the information system needs in terms of data flows, transformations of that data, and what data needs to be stored and output to achieve the objectives of the appropriate business system. The model is not constrained by the present sequence or location of the current operations, nor is it limited by the possible implementation environment. The analyst will not have embodied any assumptions about how the system is to work.

The Data Flow Diagrams are supported by a Data Dictionary containing the detailed definitions of the processes, flows and stores shown on the diagram. A continuous line may be superimposed on the Data Flow Diagram to represent the boundary of the computer system.

The system boundary explicitly shows the scope of the proposed computer system. This is very powerful because it is often the boundary of the application that causes most confusion with users and clients. Furthermore the position of the boundary also establishes the inputs and outputs of the system. Outward data flows cutting the boundary line represent the outputs of the system; inward data flows, the inputs. Clearly different boundaries of automation will lead to different inputs, outputs and supporting technologies.

The system boundary will have been established by the Authority (Client or Customer) in the transition from current to required logical systems. This will have been achieved by reviewing the Requirements List and agreeing those to be included in the proposed system – see *Introducing Systems Analysis*.

2.3 Output contents

The point has already been made that the contents of the outputs will be defined in the Data Dictionary. However, not all reports can be explicitly shown on the Data Flow Diagram and so it is useful to briefly review a number of report types that are likely to be found in most systems.

- **On demand reports**. These are usually produced to satisfy *ad hoc* queries about data stored in the system. Users may especially benefit from report generators. These allow the user to define what fields they want on a report, the criteria for record selection and the order of record printing. This relieves the analyst of the task of specifying all such requirements in advance as well as allowing the reporting system to change and reflect new user requirements.
- **Summary reports**. Some reports only give the totals from the detailed listings of individual data records. Such reports may be produced at specific intervals and so may not be up to date when used near the due date of the next generation. An Aged Debtor Report is a summary of the outstanding amounts owed by customers of a company. It is usually only completely accurate for a short time (until the next cheque arrives!).
- **Exception reports**. These reports assist decision-making by including only data items that are extraordinary in some way. Their purpose is to prompt some action or procedure. Many data values can be considered normal, acceptable or predictable and the inclusion of such values in a report only confuses the recipient. Exception reports only show data items that have exceeded a limit (below a stock re-order level), or are unexpected in a way that demands investigation or action. For example, an Outstanding Debtor Report might show all invoices that are due but have not been paid within the normal period of business credit. The design is more flexible if the exception criteria can be varied. For example, the normal period of credit might be reduced from 30 days to 15 days during a recessionary period.
- **Internal reports**. Some reports contain detailed information but are not used outside the organization and so the promotion of the company image is not important. Some outputs act as files for answering queries by those who cannot access the data directly, for example – a price list. The production of such internal reports frequently triggers further operational processes. For example, a Coin Analysis from a payroll system will give the wages clerk the information needed to request the amount of money in the correct denomination from the bank.

- **External documents**. System outputs such as customer invoices and rate demands are generated from the internal data but are used outside the organization. In such cases it is difficult to ask the recipient whether the design is understandable and usable.
- **Archival documents**. Some reports are produced when the appropriate data is no longer required on the system. For example the details of a dead person's medical records may be output on paper or microfiche for research purposes. Similarly, reports of historical financial transactions may be required for company taxation purposes.

2.4 Output technology

Output technology is usually limited to hard-copy (printers, plotters, Computer Output onto Microfilm [COM]), transient images (screens) and other media (files, disk, tape).

Selection issues will include:

- **Quality of the output required**. This will concern print quality, screen resolution and print and screen colour.
- **Volume of the output**. Printer and plotter speed will have to be considered in high volume applications.
- **Location of the output**. Certain working environments may be very noisy or create dust and dirt harmful to the machines.
- **Ease of use**. This will include ease of changing paper, fixing faults, changing font sizes, etc.
- **Specialized requirements**. Certain types of screens may be required in certain circumstances; for example, A4 size for word processing, screen scramblers for Defence applications.
- **Customer requirements**. Customers may specify that they require inputs in a certain way (e.g. supplier orders through Electronic Data Interchange (EDI)) or in a certain format (BACs tapes).
- **Interface with other systems**. Other internal systems may need the data to be produced in a certain way or may already make data available for our own system in a particular media or format.
- **Cost**. Clearly functionality and features of the output device have to be balanced against its cost.

2.5 Detailed output design

Draft layouts of outputs can be made on special paper charts or directly on a screen using some form of painting and formatting software. The latter is much more effective as the user can quickly appreciate the contents and aesthetics of the displayed information because it is in the medium that will be used in the final system. It also permits much easier amendment of layouts and this is particularly useful if the user is present and able to discuss fine details of position and vocabulary. The extensive formatting facilities of spreadsheets also make them ideal for the presentation of 'mock-up' layouts. Fourth Generation Languages (4GLS) and CASE tools (see chapter 4) also permit rapid prototyping of outputs.

The contents of the forms and reports will be defined in the supporting Data Dictionary definition. Certain other data items may be added to reflect issues not directly relevant to the user, e.g.:

- legal requirements, VAT no.;
- standard contents, company name, terms of business, etc.;
- control contents: check digits, check totals;
- standards requirements;
- security control – distribution, filing and disposal method.

There are two types of data items on any report. Fixed-data items consist of headings, descriptions of data items and instructions for the user. Variable items are data values retrieved or computed from the stored or input data. Some variable data items may be derived from other data items as the system produces the report.

Information generally has to be presented in some specified order; for example, numerical, chronological or alphabetical. This sequence allows easy searching and browsing, particularly if the report extends over several pages. Reading lengthy listings is easier if the importance of the data items is reflected in the order of presentation. A report showing debtors in declining size of debt is more immediate than one given in alphabetical order.

Readability and understanding will be enhanced if a report is marked with clearly identifiable blocks of data, separated by space for emphasis. A new block of data will correspond to a change in the value of a key data item. It may also be separated by a sub-total for the preceding block. The unprinted space also enhances the presentation. Attention should also be paid to any proposed manual filing. Space should be left at the top or the left of the page to prevent data being lost through holes being punched in the printed data or hidden in binder margins.

Three further guidelines for presentation and layout will assist in the design of effective inputs and outputs.

- **Familiarity and consistency.** Information should always be presented in a consistent and accessible way. Familiarity of style and format will promote quicker acceptance of a new report and less misunderstanding of the content. Related reports should have a familiar format so that key information can always be found in the same location on the form. Communication is enhanced by a 'house style' for such aspects as headers, typefaces and logos. This can be documented in the Standards or Style Guide (see chapter 3) where it is accessible to new members of staff who will need guidance on such issues.
- **Alignment and spacing.** Alignment of both fixed and variable data will contribute to ease of understanding and use. Numeric values should be aligned at their decimal points and character fields left aligned. Negative numerical data should be right aligned and use a suffix or brackets:

1548.24– OR (1548.24)

■ **Informative headings**. A report, form or display always requires a clear useful title that can be repeated on all subsequent pages of the document. The pages should be numbered to allow easy reference and re-collation of a dropped report. Meaningful column headings are often difficult to fit in but it is wise not to abbreviate them excessively and so leave their interpretation in doubt.

Figure 2.1 shows the basic principles of good output design.

2.6 Input design

The capture and preparation of data for input is often considered as an afterthought to the actual processing of data, but a systems design cannot be considered complete unless proper attention has been given to data entry. There is a wide variety of methods of recording input data, and the choice between them depends on the application involved, the overall system timing requirements, the volumes of data to be processed, and equipment costs and benefits.

Before considering the actual hardware that could be used for capturing input, a number of general points should be noted. The possible input methods must be reconciled with the operating requirements of the user. Furthermore, the entry of data and the receipt of output may be the only contact that the majority of employees in a company have with the computer. If the supply of data input is seen as a tedious and unrewarding activity, it is likely that the quality of the information provided will suffer.

Input is expensive. Every effort should be made to make data capture as unobtrusive as possible, a by-product of the data provider's normal activity rather than an irritating distraction from 'real work'.

The general objective of data capture is to collect and convert the data into machine-readable form with the minimum delay, minimum introduction of errors and at minimum cost.

The system boundary will again establish the inputs of the system. Incoming data flows that cut the boundary are the inputs of the system and their contents are held in a Data Dictionary. These are the data items that have to be captured through an appropriate input medium. A typical input Data Dictionary entry is shown in figure 2.2.

2.7 Input design guidelines

The selection of an appropriate input technology will be guided by:

■ the type of data being entered;
■ the frequency of data entry;
■ environmental conditions.

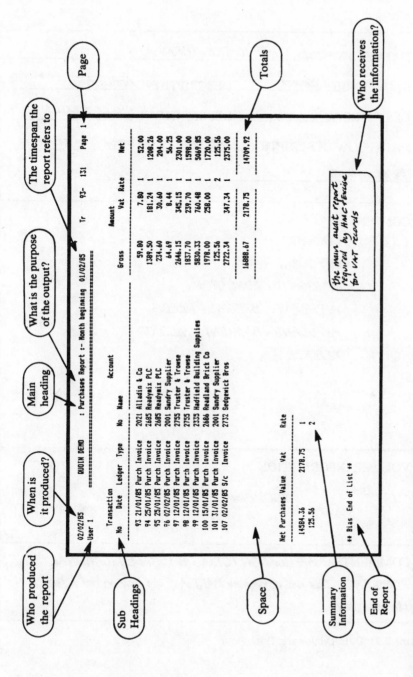

Figure 2.1 Output design factors and features.

DATA FLOW NAME: _APPLICATION-FORM-A_

SOURCE REF: _Source_   DESCRIPTION _APPLICANT_

DESTIN REF: _1_   DESCRIPTION _CHECK STATUS_

DATA FLOW DESCRIPTION _Describes an application form submitted_

by an applicant

CONTENT:

COURSE

APPLICANT

APPLICANT - EDUCATION

APPLICANT - SPECIAL - NEEDS

APPLICANT - PAYMENT - METHOD

REFEREE

VOLUME INFORMATION

2000/Year

COMMENTS   _APPLICATION FORM - B 15 The EDUCATIONAL_
REFERENCE. This will accompany PART A if the flow occurs before
the 16th July

Figure 2.2 Data Dictionary: Data Flow.

The following three guidelines may assist a developer in the evaluation of input alternatives:

- **Seek to minimize data transcription**. Every time that data is transcribed or copied the chance of error and delay is increased. Data preparation staff transcribing data from a survey form (human readable) to magnetic disc (machine readable) incur cost and delay. There will also be transcription errors as the data is copied and so procedures will have to be designed to locate these errors. This leads to further expense and delay.
- **Attempt to minimize data transmission or communication**. In data capture procedures each transmission, whether by word of mouth, post or telephone line, incurs cost, delay and an increased chance of error. The cost of transmitting data along telephone lines may be an important consideration in the design of a computer-based system. If the cost is significant it may be advantageous to place processors at a number of locations with only limited interaction between these local processors and the organization's main computer. For example, summaries of stock transactions may be despatched weekly rather than posting individual transactions to a geographically remote computer.
- **Strive to minimize the amount of data recorded**. Designers should use their prior knowledge of the characteristics of the system to reduce the burden placed on the data provider. A request, for example, for payment of water rates can print or code data about the user's name, address, postal code, property reference and payment required. The data provider's only action is to pay the bill! The same principle applies to a bank cheque transaction where the data concerning branch, account and cheque number is already recorded in a sequence of codes and the only data collection required is the amount of the cheque – the only variable data. The opportunity to code or print known data items varies from system to system but the designer should seek such opportunities because every additional data item required from the data provider increases the chance of error in the collected data. The use of turnaround documents greatly reduces input errors and volumes.

2.8 Input technologies

Input devices fall into two distinct categories. One uses keyboard transcription where data is transferred from 'human readable' to 'machine readable' form by some form of keyboard input, the other is concerned with direct input into the computer.

Keyboard transcription includes the traditional task of data preparation where the operator takes clerical documents and transcribes data onto a suitable computer media. Data entered in this way must be subjected to some kind of verification and validation. Verification is usually achieved by transcribing the data twice and investigating any discrepancies. Validation is likely to be the task of a specially written data validation program that examines incoming data and rejects entries that do not conform to an expected value range or format. The rules for validation are stored in the Data Dictionary.

Devices that permit direct entry of data into the computer eliminate transcription errors completely.

Direct input methods include:

- **Optical Character Recognition (OCR).** This technique is widely used in insurance premium notices, public utility billing and hire-purchase agreements. Documents are pre-printed with a certain font and, on return, are passed through an OCR reader. Hand-written values can also be recognized, particularly if there are printed within defined boxes on the form.
- **Magnetic Ink Character Recognition (MICR).** This is used mainly in the banking industry with the characteristic font found in every cheque book. The ability to pre-record data (about account, bank and cheque) is again exploited.
- **Optical Mark Recognition (OMR).** Readers recognize hand or machine printed marks on forms. Current devices are not limited to pencil marks but can interpret any dense mark; biro, typewriter, etc. OMR is used in multiple choice questions and lottery tickets. It demands that the application is fairly stable so that the OMR form does not have to be regularly updated.
- **Badges, tags and cards.** Swipe cards, smart cards and Kimball tags again use pre-recorded data. The latter tag is used in the clothing industry and is removed from the garment upon sale. It resembles a small punched card and it is used to store information about the garment – type, size, etc. This information can again be pre-recorded at the time of manufacture, a shirt does not change into a skirt overnight, nor does it grow into a larger size as it gets older!
- **Bar codes.** Bar codes also use the principle of recording information at the time of manufacture rather than at the point of sale. Products have standard bar codes and their suitability to clean, stable environments make them ideal for book and borrower identification in library systems.
- **Other computer media or technology.** These 0include magnetic tape, electronic messages and signals.
- **Voice input.**

Every opportunity should be taken to exploit direct input devices. These technologies are becoming cheaper, more reliable and widespread.

2.9 Summary

Output and input design is a suitable starting point for the design task. Inputs and outputs are identified from the system boundary imposed on the Data Flow Diagram. The contents of these flows is defined in the supporting Data Dictionary. An appropriate technology must be allocated to inputs and outputs taking into account system constraints, volumes and cost. The detailed design of inputs and outputs involves form, report, document and screen design. Aesthetic issues affect this detailed design and layout has many subjective elements. These can be explored with the user, particularly if the developer uses a screen and report generator offered by a Fourth Generation Language or CASE tool.

3 Designing Interfaces

3.1 Introduction

Chapter 2 gave some guidance on the task of designing inward and outward data flows, highlighting the reports that provide information for the users who undertake business tasks and the forms that capture the required raw data for this output. The logical content of these system inputs and outputs were identified from where the data flows crossed the agreed system boundary. The developer now needs to define the computer procedures to capture data and display and print output. This is the task of human–computer interface design, a task that includes designing screen displays and dialogues or conversations to link them together (Schott and Olson, 1988).

This chapter will discuss the importance of the effective design of the human–computer interface and sets out criteria against which a dialogue design may be evaluated. The components of the dialogue are introduced and three approaches to modelling the interface are presented. A human–computer dialogue may be defined as:

> an exchange of information governed by agreed conventions which takes place between a computer-based system and its users via an interactive terminal.
>
> (Coats and Vlaeminke, 1988)

A dialogue consists of a set of procedures for the exchange of information between the user and the computer. The appropriate commands and responses provide the mechanism for executing the processes provided by the system and required by the user. The structure of the dialogue will control the interaction between the user and computer and determine how information is presented and received. A dialogue may vary in this degree of control from user-initiated (where the user is in command) to computer-initiated (where the user simply responds to the requests of the system).

In general a dialogue needs to:

■ determine what task/process the user requires the system to undertake;

- obtain the data input from the user and make this available in a suitable format to the required computer task/process;
- command the computer task/process to be performed;
- receive data output from the computer task/process and present it to the user in the appropriate format.

Conventions for undertaking these tasks are as important in a human–computer dialogue as they are in normal everyday conversation. Participants in a conversation must normally use the same language, take turns to speak, listen while the other person speaks, and respond to information supplied by the other. These conventions enable everyday conversations to be effective and generally lead to the required actions resulting from clearly stated instructions or commands. However, if commands are ambiguous, mumbled or incomplete then the message becomes garbled and the resulting actions incorrect and unpredictable. The same principles of clarity are required of a human–computer dialogue – ambiguity and incompleteness will lead to mistakes and uncertainty.

Computer systems are important tools that assist the performance of many critical tasks in the management and operation of the enterprise. The human–computer dialogue is the vehicle by which this assistance takes place. To most users the dialogue is the system! Ambiguities and difficulties in the dialogue cause problems in training and operation and lead to systems underperforming. For example, a clerk who has problems entering data because of a poor screen design is likely to make more transcription errors. Similarly, a manager who wishes to display the latest sales forecasts may be frustrated by problems in obtaining that information (through poor menu design) and confused by the results that appear (due to a complicated screen layout). The clerk will have to tolerate such poor design features but will perform the task inefficiently. However, the manager is a discretionary user of the system and the lack of his or her support and use of the system will reduce the chances of achieving a successful implementation.

To be effective a dialogue has to be both functional and usable:

- **Functionality**. This is concerned with ensuring that all the required data has a mechanism for input and output. Hence dialogues have been designed for each interface defined in the Data Flow Diagram and each dialogue is complete in that it captures or displays all the data required in the input or output.
- **Usability should reinforce functionality.**

Operators of the system should be given a dialogue that is:

- **Natural**. An effective dialogue does not cause the user to significantly alter his or her approach to the task in order to interact with the computer system. A dialogue should use the vocabulary of the user in preference to one that reflects the operation of the system. Coats and Vlaeminke (1988) give a good example of this:

A designer might consider the task to be 'updating the expense file', but if users call it 'posting P47s' that is how the dialogue should refer to it.

Naturalness can also be reflected in the order in which a dialogue requests the entry of information. This should acknowledge the order in which data becomes available to the user and so not require any sorting or re-arrangement of data. Hence logical order of data entry is very important and this is one of the tasks of the Logical Dialogue Outline examined later in this chapter.

■ **Consistent.** Expectations about the way that the system will perform and react are important. Arbitrary changes in phrasing, format and layout cause frustration and anxiety. For example, a user will reasonably expect a dialogue to display help and error messages in the same area of the screen no matter which part of the system is currently being used. Furthermore, users often take their knowledge from one application to another and expect related systems to behave in a similar manner. Many difficulties have been caused by commands such as quit and exit having different consequences in different systems. Obviously the design cannot be consistent with all systems in existence, but consistency with common conventions and industry standard practices is advisable.

One of the benefits of the Windows interface is its consistency across applications, allowing regular users to be in familiar territory when using new application software running in that environment. Microsoft (1992) have published interface guidelines so that developers can create standard interfaces in their software. The purpose of the guide is to 'Promote visual and functional consistency within and across Windows-based applications'. Consistency allows users to move from one application to another with ease and speed. It minimizes the need for training and increases productivity. It also 'gives users a sense of stability, which increases their confidence in the reliability of an application and in all applications with the same interface'. An interface Style Guide is essential for ensuring consistency.

■ **Not redundant.** The data flow model should ensure that redundant data does not appear in the design. Default values (where the expected response is provided by the system for the user's confirmation) should be used wherever possible to reduce the actual keystrokes required. Derived data should always be produced by the system not by the operator.

■ **Supportive.** Many systems provide help facilities designed to aid the operator undertake an operation or correct an error. Such assistance should not be provided indiscriminately. The possibility of turning help facilities on and off will assist the new user still learning the system, the infrequent user who simply needs reminding and the frequent experienced operator who will prefer not to have the screen filled with explanatory messages. Help screens should be relevant and sensitive to the context of the difficulty.

Reporting operational errors is normally achieved by displaying appropriate messages at particular points in the dialogue. These error messages need to state exactly what is wrong and also give specific instruction in the corrective action necessary. Just reporting the error (data type mismatch) is insufficient.

The interface also needs to be escapable in that it offers users a very clear exit route. If it does not then users will find an alternative (usually switching off and subsequently denying it!)

■ **Flexible**. Finally a dialogue should be able to cater for or tolerate different levels of user knowledge and performance. There is usually more than one way to perform a task and hence dialogues must be designed to accept variations in the way a user converses with it. Many systems provide command or coded fastpaths allowing experienced users to go directly to the required function of the system. The Windows interface allows users the option of using 'alt' and the underscored letter (for example, 'alt-V' is 'View' in Microsoft Word) as an alternative to pointing and clicking with the mouse.

3.2 Dialogue types

There are four main ways of structuring the dialogue.

3.2.1 Menus

Menus present a selection of the possible options at certain stages in the dialogue. Users select a particular option by giving the appropriate letter or number or by selecting an icon with a keyboard highlight or a mouse. Many systems use permanently displayed or 'pull down' menus within a dialogue.

The main advantage of this style of interface is that it requires few keyboard skills and hence is ideal for the inexperienced or infrequent user. It is also applicable to circumstances where no specialized knowledge or training can be given or assumed. Error rates with menu dialogues are generally low and the system is effective even if the user is frequently interrupted or distracted.

However, menus may be intolerably slow for experienced users. Consequently, the design of the menus should offer flexible paths around the system and so provide short-cuts to normal routes. This can cut down the irritation of experienced users.

Menus also demand that the system inputs can be explicitly predicted and that the range of predictions is relatively small. Menu screens should be restricted to about 7–10 options with further menus called from some (or perhaps all) of these options. It is also unwise to exceed more than three levels of menu. Excessively deep menus lead to users becoming confused about their current position in the system.

The Windows interface permits a large number of menu options without apparent over-crowding of the screen. The first menu is essentially an icon set with users selecting an option by using the screen pointer and double clicking with the mouse. However, the opening screen also has a horizontal text-based menu, each option of which leads to a pull-down menu that can be activated by screen pointing. These menus are hidden until selected. The net effect of this is to allow users to traverse a considerable number of options without leaving one physical screen. This ability to browse menus should not be underestimated. The traditional hierarchical menu created frustration when an option selected by mistake led to ponderous wasted moves up and down the hierarchy.

3.2.2 Form filling

In a 'form-filling' dialogue input data is entered onto screens that resemble a form. Areas of the screen are protected from input and the cursor is placed at relevant points to indicate where and in what order the data is to be entered.

Completion of forms is a familiar activity to many employees and systems can often be designed to match proposed or existing clerical forms. This familiarity reduces the need for training. Furthermore, a relatively large amount of data can be entered on one screen and the values of this data do not have to be predicted by the dialogue.

Certain principles of design can enhance the method:

- The data entry progresses left to right and top to bottom. This reflects the natural entry of a clerical form.
- Entry fields should be clearly delimited from displayed or retrieved data.
- The form should collect information available sat that time. It should not try to encompass data that is input at different stages or times.
- Default values should be used wherever possible. Data already available on the system should be retrieved, not re-entered.

Form filling is particularly appropriate where the dialogue demands the entry of a large number of fairly standard data items. The validation of these data items may take place during input or after a batch (usually a screenful of data has been entered). The former demands access to data files and may slow down the entry process. The latter requires a simple and effective editing facility so that users can quickly skip to fields that need re-entering.

3.2.3 Command language

In menu and form-filling modes the user has responded to a computer-initiated dialogue. However, command or direct language is user-initiated. Commands or codes that should be known to the system are directly entered from the keyboard. The system does not try to predict these commands in any way.

Command language offers little support to the user but it does provide a precise, concise dialogue that allows a considerable degree of flexibility and control. Dialogue familiarity depends on learning a wide range of commands that must be regularly rehearsed if they are not to be forgotten.

In general, command language is the least supportive dialogue structure and is most appropriate to experienced and frequent users. SQL (Structured Query Language) is a command language (Din, 1994).

```
SELECT DEPT_NO, DEPT_NAME FROM DEPARTMENTS
WHERE DEPT_NAME = 'Engineering'
```

SQL may itself be implemented as a menu-driven system where command lists are given and the user selects an appropriate command from this list. This Query-by-

Example or Query-by-Forms approach effectively transforms the interface from a command- to a menu-driven structure.

3.2.4 Natural language

The use of natural language is a relatively recent trend in dialogue design. Such dialogues are currently limited in both syntax and vocabulary and the style is generally very formal.

In practice, all the dialogue types will probably be used at different parts of the system. A menu structure might be most appropriate where the range of inputs is relatively small and all possible inputs have to be explicitly displayed. Forms are particularly suitable for input of a large set of data values taken from standard operational transactions – such as time sheets, invoices, down-time notifications, etc. Command language is appropriate where only a few input values will be required for each process and these values are taken from a limited set of easily recalled commands. Finally, Question and Answer dialogues are suitable for applications where the range of input values is too great for a menu structure, too complex for command language, or where the next question depends upon the answer to the current one. It is commonly used in particularly crucial events.

Are you sure you wish to delete these files (Yes/No): **N**

Dialogue modelling is concerned with representing the interface to users and developers. This chapter looks at three candidate models. The Logical Dialogue Outline (LDO), the Input/Output Structure, and finally the State Transition Diagram (STD).

3.3 Logical dialogue outline

SSADM Version 3 used a logical dialogue design to represent the interfaces of the system under development. This design is summarized in a Logical Dialogue Outline (LDO), which is used to show users and operators what they will be required to do in the proposed system. LDOs may be modified in physical design.

Dialogues are described in terms of

- **Initiators and terminators**. These denote the beginning and end of the dialogue and are shown as circles.
- **Logical screens**. These contain a brief statement of the content of each screen at that point. It is likely that many logical screens will make up a physical one. The logical screen is essentially a discrete step in the dialogue and it is shown as a rectangular box.
- **User decision points**. These are the points where the user can influence the direction of the dialogue. Each user decision point is shown as a triangle and is denoted by a letter. Each branch is numbered and a key to these numbers is given on the form.

■ **Routing lines.** These show the interconnection of logical screens, decision points and dialogue nodes. A routing line can also be used to show existence checks in the software. For example, product-code entry may fail because that code does not exist (an existence check failure) or because a valid but incorrect code was entered and the wrong product description has been displayed. The latter check would be represented by a user decision point, the former by a routing line loop.

■ **Dialogue nodes.** Transferring control to another dialogue described elsewhere.

The graphical representation of the dialogue is summarized with the five symbols introduced above within a Logical Dialogue Outline form that adds further comments and information.

The logical dialogue outline form requests information about access rights and dialogue volumes. There are four main columns within the form itself:

■ **Logical screens.** These show the detail of the graphical LDO discussed in the previous section.

■ **Data elements.** The data elements input into the dialogue or are produced by it.

■ **Processing comments.** These clarify the purpose of the logical screens.

■ **User decisions.** These clarify the user decision options.

These may be supplemented by a Service Time column used to give the required response time associated with that part of the dialogue.

Figure 3.1 shows an Adjustment Form for the Solar Electrical system. The Logical Dialogue Outline describing the entry of this data is given as figure 3.2 and it illustrates how the diagram is essentially a flowchart of the dialogue.

3.4 Input/output structures

Dialogues in SSADM Version 4 are described in an Input/Output Structure Diagram. The contents of the data flow are first documented on an I/O Description form (figure 3.3), which plays the same role as the Data Dictionary entry for that flow. Details from this document are then transcribed onto an I/O Structure Description form. This lists both input and output data items. Attributes that are entered or displayed together are brought together in an I/O Structure element name – Adjustment Header and Adjustment Summary are the two examples in Figure 3.4.

The I/O Structure Descriptions are then converted into I/O Structure Diagrams using a standard Jackson-like notation. The bottom leaves of the structure represent one or more data items crossing the system boundary and each is annotated as either an input or an output. Within the I/O structure:

■ Repeating groups of data items are represented as an iteration.

■ Optional groups of data items are represented by a selection with a null option.

■ Mutually exclusive groups are represented as options under a selection.

SOLAR ELECTRICAL
Date : 24/11/90

ADJUSTMENT
FORM No: 122

Product code	Product description	Adj. code	Adj. reason	Qty
01816	Multiman	Ø	Delivery	60
01813	Tefal deep-fat fryer	Ø	Delivery	100
01813	Tefal deep-fat fryer	1	Damage	2

SIGNATURE L Jones

Figure 3.1 Adjustment form.

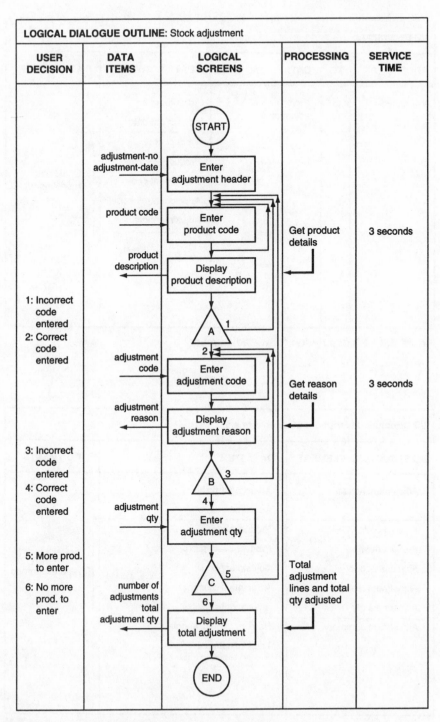

Figure 3.2 Logical dialogue outline for adjustment.

I/O Description				
FROM	**TO**	**DATA FLOW NAME**	**DATA CONTENT**	**COMMENTS**
Warehouse	6	Stock adjustment	Adjustment-no Adjustment-date Product-code Product-description Adjustment-code Adjustment-reason Adjustment-qty	Could be a repeating group

Figure 3.3 I/O description form – adjustment.

I/O Structure description: Stock adjustment		
I/O STRUCTURE ELEMENT	**DATA ITEM**	**COMMENTS**
Adjustment header	Adjustment-no Adjustment-date	
Product code Product details Adjustment code Adjustment reason Adjustment qty	Product-code Product-description Adjustment-code Adjustment-reason Adjustment-qty	Could be a repeating group
Adjustment summary	Number of adjustments Total adjustment	

Figure 3.4 I/O structure description form – adjustment.

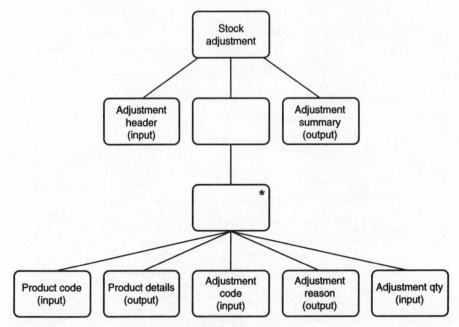

Figure 3.5   Input/output structure diagram: adjustment.

Figure 3.5 shows the Input/Output Structure Diagram for Stock Adjustment. Notice the use of empty boxes to preserve the structure. The iteration is essentially the same as the loop from user decision box C in the Logical Dialogue Outline.

3.5 State transition diagrams

State Transition Diagrams are particularly effective for describing control transformations and so may be applied to dialogue structures.

The diagram comprises four components

- **The state**. This is represented by a soft box. The dialogue is in only one state at a given time. One of the states on the diagram is designated as the initial state and is shown by a transition arrow into the state with no source state. This initial state is the behaviour of the system before any transitions have occurred.

   One or more states on the diagram may be designated as final states. A final state has transition arrows entering but no transition arrows to other states.

   The state represents the dialogue at a discrete point in time. The events that cause transitions in state are instantaneous – there is no slow, continuous change in a dialogue.
- **Transitions**. The transition is represented as an arrow. It shows the movement from one state to another. Transitions can exist between any state and any other state, including the state from which the transition started. Multiple transitions to and from a given state are allowed.

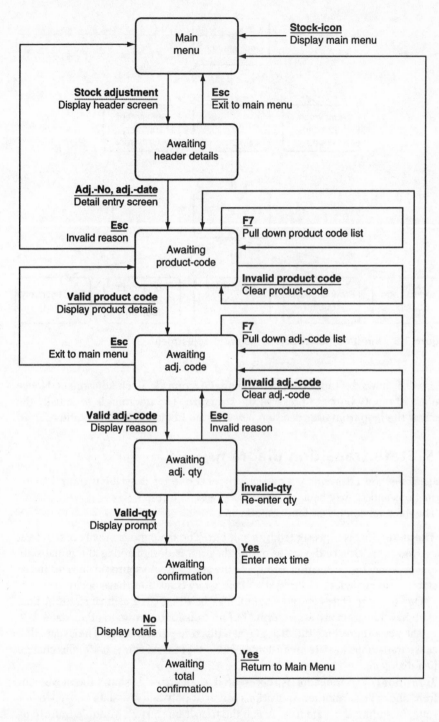

Figure 3.6 State transition diagram: adjustment.

■ **Conditions cause the system to make a transition.** The condition is written above a line that separates the condition and action of the transition.

■ **Actions are what happens when the transition occurs.** Several independent actions may be taken on a single transition. They are all assumed to take place simultaneously unless an explicit sequence is indicated.

In formal terms this notation defines a finite automaton with output. The State Transition Diagram for Stock Adjustment is given in figure 3.6. Main menu is the initial state of this diagram.

3.6 Summary

This chapter has examined basic design issues in the interface. Users are increasingly expecting a W(indows) I(con) M(ouse) P(ull-down lists/menus) or G(raphical) U(ser) I(nterface) that works consistently with their other workstation applications – such as word processing and spreadsheets. The increased use of client–server solutions will reinforce this trend and bring about the end of TP driven screen at a time processing. Opportunities also exist for re-packaging legacy systems with a new 'front-end' written in a language such as Visual Basic to present a new and consistent look to a functional but outdated system.

These opportunities demand careful control. Most methodologies suggest the development of Interface Style Guides that document use of function keys, screen layouts, report layouts, HELP messages and location, etc. The Microsoft guide provides an international standard and certainly seems a good starting point for any internal Style Guide.

The increased variety of the interface also makes demands upon the models used to communicate and document its structure. The Logical Dialogue Outline is a flowchart of the dialogue. We use it to on occasions to ensure logical order and consistency with clerical forms and documents. It was poorly documented in SSADM Version 3 and hence under-used. Its successor the Input/Output Structure Diagram is less accessible to users but (in SSADM) now forms the basis of later enquiry process design (see Skidmore *et al.*, 1995). We first used the State Transition Diagram to allow users to easily see their escape points in a system. We have found it helpful in describing Windows type interfaces and have included it in user manuals where it certainly saves a thousand words!

4 Rapid Application Development

4.1 Introduction

The Systems Development Life Cycle (SDLC) is usually characterized by phases and deliverables. The actual stages, steps and deliverables of systems development will vary depending on the size of the proposed system, the type of work involved, the approved standards and project management.

In the past two decades the SDLC has been enhanced by adopting new methods and techniques. These have been primarily aimed at improving communication (using graphical notation rather than text) and progression (moving seamlessly from analysis models, through design, to program specifications). However, it has been suggested that these improvements do not eliminate the inherent weaknesses of this approach. The models still remain too abstract and too difficult for users to comprehend. It has also been argued that they take too long to produce. By the time they have been completed the business operations and requirements have changed.

Prototypes have been mentioned in the literature for nearly twenty years (see, for example, Basili and Turner, 1975). The approach has some attraction because for many industries 'the building of a prototype has long been regarded as a necessary step in any development activity' (Dearnley and Mayhew, 1983). The prototype, in the literature, is defined as a working system: 'a model is regarded as a pictorial representation, whereas a prototype is a system that actually works'.

Lantz has suggested a prototyping methodology (Lantz, 1984). which includes structured specification models such as Data Flow Diagrams and a normalized Entity Relationship Model as well as prototypes. He recognized that many people in information systems management have viewed prototyping as a 'quick and dirty' approach talented people use for urgent systems projects. These people often seem to be 'winging it', when they're prototyping, taking short cuts that eliminate unnecessary steps in the systems development process. Unfortunately the 'winging' and the results of 'winging' are not recorded and hence the knowledge cannot be re-used in the systematic way.

Rapid Application Development (RAD) is an approach to software development popularized by James Martin (1984). It is formally defined within Information Engineering and uses many of the formal models and techniques defined within the full-blown method. It also has four key elements;

■ prototyping;
■ Computer Aided Software Engineering (CASE);
■ Joint Application Development (JAD);
■ skilled small team development.

This chapter primarily considers prototyping and CASE. However, JAD and skilled small-team development are also briefly touched upon.

4.2 Prototyping: meaning and procedure

Websters Dictionary defines the word prototype as:

■ An original model on which something is patterned: an archetype.
■ An individual that exhibits the essential features of a later type.
■ A standard or typical example.

The first definition is closest to that of manufacturing, where a prototype frequently proceeds the fabrication process. This is not usually appropriate to information systems development (except perhaps, for a software house releasing a new product). The second definition, a system that captures the essential features of a later system, is the most appropriate definition of an information system prototype. A prototype system is intentionally incomplete. It will be subsequently modified, expanded, supplemented or supplanted.

In their seminal article, Naumann and Jenkins define prototyping as a four step procedure (Naumann and Jenkins, 1982):

■ **Identify the user's basic information requirements**. Two distinct emphases are suggested for this approach. The 'Data abstracting approach' and the 'Process simulating approach'. Data abstraction was the focus of the CADIS Research Group that suggested an 'infological simulation' in the form of experiments with a database-driven pilot system. In this view, determining requirements means constructing a model of the relevant data. Systems design begins with identification of entities, attributes and data structures. This approach is also identifiable in recent object-oriented approaches where generic models are used to establish a framework for the systems development. The material covered in chapters 5 and 7 is relevant to this approach.

The other view is that the first step in prototyping is to model the process. Basili and Turner (1975) suggest iterative enhancement during interaction with users. The term 'heuristic development' has been used to describe this approach. The material covered in Chapters 6 and 7 is relevant to this perspective.

However, whichever view is taken, both views agree that completeness is not important at this stage. RAD suggests that these basic information requirements are captured in a Joint Application Development (JAD) session. JAD replaces or supplements the traditional series of interviews that are associated with conventional systems analysis. JAD sessions are essentially intensive workshops attended by those in authority with the responsibility and expertise to agree requirements. The requirements are captured on a CASE tool (see later) during the meeting and are approved before it ends. The sessions are also attended by impartial facilitators who address the process of analysis and design without getting involved in design decisions. These facilitators are often well versed in the business application area (so called domain experts – see chapter 7) and so are well qualified to help prompt the clarification of enterprise rules.

■ **Develop a working prototype.** The initial prototype must be implemented in a very short time. A number of authors have suggested that this time should be two or three days. Even the most conservative of writers have suggested that prototyping or bread boarding is effective only if done in weeks rather than months or years. The time requirement serves both user and builder: 'The user has a tangible system to experience and criticise – the builder gets responses based upon that experience.'

RAD suggests that prototyping makes use of the CASE tool used in the JAD session, hence code generation facilities are an important requirement of the CASE tool selected to support RAD. The time constraints of the prototype are defined within an agreed 'timebox' (see later).

■ **Implement and use the prototype system.** Hands on experience of the system provides experience, understanding and evaluation:

> It is a live and operational system, users cannot escape and opt out so easily. Users and managers, once they realize that things can be changed and that they can exert influence, may in turn participate with more dedication.

■ **Revise and enhance the prototype system.** Undesirable or missing features identified by the user must be corrected. Rapid turnaround remains important, and several iterations will be required until the system is complete.

4.3 Prototype construction

Most authors distinguish between 'throw-it-away' and 'incremental' prototyping. In the latter instance the prototype undergoes a number of refining cycles until it becomes the final system. Using non-CASE generated code this will require some development of error trapping and recovery routines. Re-programming of 'working' code may also be needed to reflect internal standards of naming and modularity. The prototype may have been constructed using value rather than parameter passing and temporary data files. These areas will obviously have to be re-addressed.

RAD favours incremental development. However, this incremental approach should preferably be implemented through the CASE models, not the code itself. It is the models that are developed, modified and enhanced. Code is then generated from these models. This clearly gives a much cleaner approach to prototyping.

Throw-it-away prototyping requires the re-coding of the entire system. The prototype may have been developed with the prime aim of defining user requirements. The software used to do this may turn out to be inadequate beyond a certain volume of transactions. The re-coding is required to permit the phasing out of the prototype. Furthermore the target language of the final system may be different to that used to construct the prototype. Prototypes are thrown away, not developed on into the final system.

Grady Booch (1994) suggests that development taking place at the broad (macro) level and at the detailed (micro) level. *Conceptualization* establishes the broad requirements of the system. Prototypes are the primary products of conceptualization, a quick and dirty 'proof of concept'. However, 'such prototypes are by their very nature incomplete and only marginally engineered'. He goes on to say that 'it must be emphasized that all such prototypes are meant to be thrown away'.

Lantz (1984) calls this throw it away method the 'mock-up' approach to prototyping. He summarizes his view of the advantages of these two approaches in the table 4.1.

Whichever approach is adopted it must be clear that the system has to be written in very powerful and flexible software that permits programs to be created very quickly as well as allowing easy coding of extensions and amendments. Conventional programming languages (such as COBOL) are not well suited for this type of development. Prototyping requires powerful software tools that allow the relatively inexpensive building of systems that might eventually be discarded.

Table 4.1 Full and mock-up prototyping compared (from Lantz)

Advantage	Full prototype	Prototype as mock-up
System meets user's needs	x	x
User participates in design	x	x
Early discovery of design problems	x	x
Requirements are developed experimentally not theoretically	x	x
User participates in development	x	
System interface problems must be solved from the start	x	
Work of several phases concurrent with development	x	
Excessive documentation not needed	x	x
Unexpected problems that consume major amounts of time don't occur	x	
Much user training a by-product of development	x	

Source: Lantz (1984).

Candidate tools are explained below.

4.3.1 Application packages

It may be possible to develop a demonstration system using an appropriate package and to let the user identify problems, possibilities and opportunities using the package as a yardstick. It is often easier to say what is inadequate about, say a production control package, than it is to define requirements in the abstract. In this instance the application package is playing the role of a generic model.

4.3.2 Program generators

Program Generators have been available for a number of years and a variety of different types may be identified. One sort uses a question and answer English dialogue to produce the program logic which it then encodes in a High Level language such as BASIC or COBOL. A different type adopts a screen-based approach where the designer effectively paints the screen by typing directly on to it. Once satisfied with the display, the Program Generator is invoked to automatically produce the code required to produce that screen. It may also produce validation routines stopping only to request what type and range of data is required in a certain field and what error message should appear when the user makes a mistake. These may be produced directly if the Program Generator has access to a Data Dictionary.

4.3.3 Reusable code

Many systems are conceptually similar. Tasks frequently re-appear – menu design, password protection, print routines, date checking, etc. It is possible to build up a library of well-proven, well-documented routines that may be plugged together to make up a system. The content, not the logic, will need changing and some development will be required to make a complete system. However, access to a store of well-tested standard modules should ease development and maintenance. Many information system departments produce, document and publish such modules to encourage internal re-use. Re-usability of proven code is a key theme of object-oriented development. Prototypes can either be constructed from the proven object set, or construction time is reduced because development is concerned with changing objects that are known to work in the first place.

4.3.4 Published objects and library sets

PC development languages increasingly have published object and library sets that can be purchased and plugged into a specific tailored system. Examples include generic facilities, such as calculators and browsers and application objects, such as invoices and despatch notes. Thus development begins to resemble assembly, using both internally and externally produced objects.

4.3.5 CASE tools

It is with CASE tools that prototyping becomes particularly effective. The facility of some CASE tools to generate code means that the maintenance of the software is provided through the models not through the code itself. Hence code and models are always compatible. Unfortunately these CASE tools are expensive (see chapter 1) but they probably offer the most robust prototyping method.

4.3.6 Fourth generation languages

Languages may be seen as passing through three previous generations:

- **First Generation: machine code.** These instruct the machine through direct binary code, are closely associated with the architecture of the host processor and are complex to write, read and debug.
- **Second Generation: assembler languages.** Uses symbolic codes. Machine instructions are given by mnemonic alphabetic codes. These are easier to understand although still closely allied to machine architecture.
- **Third Generation: high level languages such as FORTRAN, COBOL, PL/1 and BASIC.** These are written in procedural code, are largely independent of the hardware architecture permitting portability and are much easier to use.

There is no agreed definition on what constitutes a Fourth Generation Language. A possible checklist of desirable features for 4GL evaluation (Martin, 1982) is summarized below:

- Centred around a relational database.
- Links to other proprietary databases and other non-database files. This will permit gradual transition to the new development environment.
- Integrated and active Data Dictionary.
- Simple Query Language. May use Structured Query Language (SQL) or some Query-by-Example or Query-by-Forms facility.
- Integrated Screen Design Tool.
- Dialogue Design Tool. Including generation and manipulation of business graphics.
- Report Generator.
- Procedural Coding facility. This may be done directly through a conventional language (say COBOL) or indirectly via a code Design Aid (such as an Action Diagrammer).
- Non-Procedural Programming Code. Most 4GLs have their own development language.
- Spreadsheets and graphics.
- Lantz (1984) adds the need for a tool to allow test data generation and interactive testing.

If the 4GL is to provide a complete development facility for the professional programmer, analyst and end user it must clearly have a range of tools to accommodate disparate requirements and skill levels. It must also dove-tail with the past development strategy of the organization and the systems developed under that strategy. 4GLs that require massive re-writes of current operational systems are likely to extend the development backlog, not reduce it.

Many 4GL vendors are now providing CASE 'front-ends' for their product. However, there is a subtle but important difference between prototyping with 4GLs and prototyping through a CASE tool that offers code generation. In the first instance changes in the prototype are made through changing program code. Supporting documentation and models have to be manually adjusted. There is a chance that models and code will become inconsistent. Standards and management procedures have to be specified and monitored to ensure that this does not happen. In the second instance this is not necessary because code is never directly modified. It is the models that are changed prior to automatic code generation. Models and code are always consistent.

4.4 Prototyping assessed

Lantz (1984) lists the following advantages of prototyping:

- **Pleases users**. Instead of only going to requirements meetings and walkthroughs, reviewing screens and report layouts and signing off various documents, many of which they do not fully understand, the user actively participates in the design and development of the system on a day-to-day basis. JAD sessions provide users with an active input into systems development.
- **Reduces development cost**. Gremillion (1983) suggests that total systems development costs are 25 per cent lower then costs associated with the traditional approach.
- **Prototyping decreases communication problems**. This applies to communication problems between user and information systems people, and also between those working on the new system being prototyped and those working on systems it must communicate with.
- **Lower operations costs**. Systems developed by prototyping use less computer resources. They do this because they produce less reports and screens programmed to meet the 'I think I need' requirement. Users often think they need a report or screen which, in fact, they don't use again after the system is installed. Systems developed through prototyping do not usually produce such reports and screens. Furthermore, they usually contain fewer validations and unnecessary controls.
- **Prototyping slashes the calendar time required to produce a project**. It does this by cutting staffing needs in a number of ways:
  - it doesn't require excessive documentation;
  - good communication takes less time than poor communication;
  - no last minute surprises arise requiring major modifications;
  - Much of the user training is a by-product of development, not a separate phase.

In his software experiment Boehm (1984) concluded that:

- Prototyping tended to produce a smaller product, with roughly equivalent performance using less effort. The prototyped products averaged about 40 per cent smaller than the specified products and required about 45 per cent less effort to produce. In performance, they rated somewhat lower on functionality and robustness, but somewhat higher on ease of learning and ease of use. The main reason for this effect appeared to be that the process of prototyping fostered a higher threshold for incorporating marginally useful features into the software product. The process of prototyping also gave software developers a more realistic feel for the amount of effort required to add features to a project, and the lack of definitive specification meant that prototypes were less loaded into a set of promises to deliver capabilities than the specifiers.
- Prototyping did not tend to produce higher productivity if productivity is measured in delivered source instructions per man-hour. However, if 'productivity' is measured in equivalent user satisfaction per man-hour, prototyping did tend to be superior.
- Prototyping did tend to provide a number of benefits frequently ascribed to it: These included:
  – products with better human–machine interfaces;
  – always having something that works;
  – a reduced deadline effect at the end of the project.

Lantz (1984) provides four possible disadvantages of the prototyping approach:

- There is a visible use of computer resources. Using prototyping development tools such as 4GLs and CASE expends more computer time than traditional development approaches. Some development teams are not equipped with the basic hardware and software needed for prototype development.
- The object system may be less efficient. Fourth Generation Languages and CASE tools may produce systems that consume more run-time than 3GLs and hand-coded systems.
- Requires co-operation between user and information systems. In some organizations the relationships between information systems and users have deteriorated to the point that any project requiring co-operation would be doomed from its beginning.
- Some view prototyping as an art not a methodology. If clever, talented staff prototype as a way of expressing their artfulness in implementing systems, the organization will benefit by however much work those talented people can do. But their management may rightly worry that this experience is not documented or reproducible.

Boehm's (1984) experiment suggested the following:

- The prototyping teams spent proportionally less effort planning and designing, and proportionally more time testing and fixing.
- More difficult integration occurred due to lack of interface specifications.
- A less coherent design emerged.

Alavi lists the following drawbacks (Alavi, 1984):

■ Prototypes can be oversold. Some project managers stated that by definition a prototype has limited capabilities and captures only the essential features of the operational system. Sometimes unrealistic user expectations are created by overselling the prototype, which may result in unmet user expectations and disappointment.

■ Prototypes are difficult to manage and control. Several project managers stated that due to the 'newness' and nature of prototyping, there is a lack of know-how for planning, budgeting, managing and control. Traditional life cycle approaches have specific phases and milestones and specific deliverables that are established before project initiation are used as guidelines for project planning and control. Planning and control of prototyping projects are more difficult because the form of the evolving system, the number of revisions to the prototype, and some of the user requirements are unknown at the outset. Lack of explicit planning and control guidelines may bring about a reduction in the discipline needed for proper management (i.e. documentation and testing activities may be bypassed or superficially performed).

'Timeboxing' is a concept introduced to address some of these project management issues. Timeboxing establishes objectives for the prototype and sets a restricted time for the development team to meet those objectives. Although the timebox begins with a rough idea of what the product should look like, the exact functionality of the final deliverables (developed through iteration) is less important than the fact that the prototype should meet its general objectives. In the timebox approach, the deadline is fixed and the functionality is flexible. This approach will only work if the users and developers agree to the concept and are willing to recognize that the deliverable at the end of the timebox may be reduced in scope or functionality.

Timeboxing was introduced as long ago as 1984 by DuPont for system development projects that could be done in under 90 days. They reasoned that any effort longer than 90 days would be more likely to miss business opportunities and exceed time and budget estimates. One of the originators of the technique suggests that the time constraint forces users and developers to separate a solution's essential elements from the merely desirable ones.

■ It is difficult to prototype large information systems. It is not clear how a large system should be divided for the purpose of prototyping or how aspects of the system to be prototyped are identified and boundaries set. In most cases, time and project resource constraints determine the boundaries and scope of the prototyping effort. Moreover, the internal technical arrangements of large information systems prototypes may be haphazard and inefficient and may not perform well in operational environment with large amounts of data or large numbers of users.

■ It is difficult to maintain user enthusiasm. In some cases, user involvement and interest waned after the working prototype was developed. After high priority user requirements were satisfied by the prototype, users were not willing to spend time and resources to complete and 'clean up' what was, in the minds of the designers, only an early version of the system. Instead, users wanted the design team to move on to a new project.

Alavi (1984) suggests that the prototyping effort should be undertaken by designers who are well informed about the prototyping approach and that its philosophy and plans should be understood by designers and users alike. In the laboratory experiment, designers who used prototyping reported a high level of change in user requirements compared to designers who used the life cycle approach. Frequent changes in user requirements may frustrate designers unless they are prepared to expect the change and view it positively. Prototyping is a new approach to information systems development, and like any organizational innovation, it needs a supportive organizational climate. Prerequisites to successful prototyping include technological tools that facilitate fast response to user requests and motivated and knowledgeable users and designers.

The prototyping approach might be particularly appropriate when developers are faced with unclear or ambiguous user requirements. Prototyping seems to be effective in coping with undecided users and clarifying 'fuzzy' requirements. Also, prototyping should be considered in situations where there is a need for experimentation and learning before commitment of resources to development of a full-scale system. A typical situation would be one in which innovative technical tools or approaches are used.

Merlyn (1991) suggests that RAD is especially appropriate when requirements are not well understood or easily pre-specified. He feels that this is particularly so in applications developed in 'front office' or departmental computing applications. In contrast, applications that depend upon algorithmic complexity or require significant prespecification, such as aerospace and defence systems, probably lend themselves less well to RAD methods.

He concludes that RAD offers a massive potential trap for the unwary, creating a portfolio of applications that were never conceived to work together, except in a highly complicated evolutionary fashion, without the benefit of an overall architecture.

Recent writers (Tudor and Tudor, 1994) have suggested that RAD is best applied when the project is:

- relatively small;
- limited in scope and impact on the organization;
- does not require a new or special hardware or software platform;
- uses 4GLs or CASE tools;
- implemented by practitioners highly skilled both in the use of RAD and in the development and implementation of systems in the target environment.

4.5 The development team

The final element of RAD is the need for system construction to be carried out by small teams of highly motivated people (sometimes called SWAT – skilled with advanced tools – teams) Such teams of four or five people should not take any longer than three or four elapsed months. Some authors have suggested that an organization adopting RAD should allocate its best staff to RAD projects. Certainly the RAD method must consider the:

- **Size of the team**. Research shows that small teams are more effective than large teams. A team size of between four and six is suggested. Belbin (1981) has suggestions on ideal team sizes.
- **Composition of the team**. Some authors on RAD suggest that the team should be comprised of 'high performance' individuals. However, there is a worry that this might be interpreted as teams consisting of highly intelligent individuals, as measured through standard tests or indicators such as educational qualifications. But Belbin's (1981) work on Apollo teams suggests that such teams do not perform well, and this is borne out from practical experience. His work suggests that there are complementary team roles that need to be recognized in the construction of a balanced team.

  Furthermore, research also suggests that users value experience in the organization or work environment as opposed to formal qualifications or personal attributes such as verbal fluency. This should also be taken into account in team composition.
- **Motivation within the team**. The need for highly motivated individuals is stressed by most RAD authors. However, this means that the factors that motivate employees must be well understood and implemented. Staff are not motivated by telling them that they should be.

4.6 Summary

This chapter has reviewed the meaning, implementation and possible application of prototyping. In some instances prototyping demands the construction of formal models (as in CASE) while in others it may be a quick proof of concept, which is then thrown away. In our own company we tend to use prototyping for functionality rather than data structures. Thus a formal Logical Data Model is developed but the processes across that model are explored through prototyping. We tend to use this approach when users are:

- unclear about their specific requirements;
- unable or unwilling to sign-off detailed process specifications.

However, it is also fair to say that projects using this approach have provided us with more control and change management problems than those that have used formal process specifications. If 4GLs are being used then my own preference is for 'throw away' prototypes. As one of my delegates said recently; Booch's (1994) comment on 'marginally engineered' is probably a euphemism for 'crap code'.

5 Logical Data Design

5.1 Introduction

Relational Data Analysis is a technique for deriving data structures that are robust, unambiguous, free from redundant duplication, flexible and easy to maintain. It also has the following objectives:

- to identify dependencies between data elements;
- to produce unambiguous data representations;
- to eliminate redundant duplication of data;
- to identify associations between relationships;
- to provide a basis for shared data usage.

The technique involves the application of a number of normalization rules to produce a set of normalized relations. These relations can be represented graphically as a Logical Data Structure or entity-relationship diagram.

Relational Data Analysis can be used at a number of points in the development of systems. It is introduced in this book at the point where the contents of inputs and outputs have been agreed and draft screens, forms and reports are available. However, it can also be used during requirements analysis and can be applied to the forms of the current system to help establish the entities of the business application area.

5.2 Basic concepts and terminology

Relational Data Analysis uses a tabular representation. A *relation* is a two dimensional table comprising of a number of columns and rows of data. Each column represents a data item or attribute of the relation. Each row represents a particular occurrence of that relation. Each relation is given a unique singular name.

A typical relation might be DELEGATE with the data items delegate-id, delegate-name and company-code. Typical rows are:

Delegate-id	Delegate-name	Company-code
1237894	Smith	COPO
7562952	Jones	HAGA
5419754	Smith	COPO

To be a relation the table must fit the following description.

No two rows are the same. The data item or group of data items that uniquely identify each row are known as the key or identifier. If the key contains only one data item it is known as a simple key. There may be more than one group of data items which can act as the key for the relation. These are known as candidate keys. The unique identifier of the relation (selected from one of the candidate keys) is known as its primary key. A suitable key should:

- guarantee uniqueness of the row;
- be the smallest number of columns;
- be non-textual if possible;
- not contain null values;
- be stable.

The key field may be shown by underlining or emboldening:

Delegate-id, delegate-name, company-code

The ordering of the columns and the rows is not significant.

Columns (data items) can be interchanged without affecting the information held by the relation. Each column should have a unique name. If row order is significant (for example, delegates held in order of age) then there is some meaning to the sequence and hence data is missing from the relation. Date-of-birth may be added to allow rearrangement of the rows.

Delegate-id, delegate-name, company-code, date-of-birth

In addition, for a relation to be normalized, all attributes should be *atomic* – each row/column intersection must only contain a single attribute value.

The sole primary key of one relation may also appear as an attribute in another one. For example company-id is also the identifier of the relation COMPANY.

COMPANY
Company-code, company-name, company-address

Company-code is known as a *foreign key* in DELEGATE and is marked with an asterisk.

Delegate-id, delegate-name, *company-code, date-of-birth

Where a foreign key is part of the identifier of another relation it is not conventionally marked with an asterisk.

Company-code, Area-code, salesperson, orders-year-to-date

The principles of functional dependency and determinants are also relevant to normalization. This was considered in *Introducing Systems Analysis* and is summarized below:

Functional dependency: An attribute Y of a relation R is functionally dependent on another attribute X of R if and only if each value of X is associated with only one value of Y. For example, employee-name is usually functionally dependent upon employee-number. Employee number is said to be the *determinant* of employee-name.

5.3 Bottom-up normalization

This section shows how the relations of a system may be developed from the forms, reports and screens of the required logical model.

Figure 5.1 shows a context diagram for a very limited project recording system. There are only three inputs and outputs for this system and examples of these are given in figures 5.2, 5.3 and 5.4. The task is to produce the best data structure for this system given the contents of these three forms and reports.

The 'bottom-up' approach to normalization achieves this by normalizing each form, report and screen individually and then rationalizing the results at the end of the procedure.

Normalization begins by listing the attributes in their order on the form. For the Machine Requirements List (figure 5.2) the unnormalized (UNF) data item listing is as follows;

> **Project-code**
> Project-description
> Project-location
> Machine-code
> Machine-type
> Machine-cost
> Date-required
> Duration

The first data item can be marked as a candidate key for the whole relation.

First Normal Form removes repeating groups to create new relations. Repeating groups are found by posing the following question:

Is there only one value of each non-key attribute for each data value of the key?

So, for example, given a value of project-code (p1) is there only one value of project-description? From the form (figure 5.2) the answer appears to be yes – hospital.

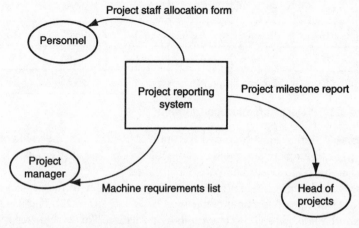

Figure 5.1 Context diagram of a project reporting system.

Project-code	Project-desc.	Project-location	Machine-code	Machine-type	Machine-cost	Date-required	Duration
p1	hospital	London	m5	dumper	200	21/1/88	15
			m7	dumper	200	25/1/88	4
			m12	crane	1000	3/2/88	20
p4	car-park	Leeds	m6	mixer	300	4/3/88	10
			m7	dumper	200	12/3/88	5
			m12	crane	1000	1/4/88	1
p5	hospital	Cambridge	m7	dumper	200	1/7/88	3
			m11	mixer	300	3/8/88	5

Figure 5.2 Machine requirements list.

PROJECT CODE: ISC001

PROJECT TYPE: NEW DEVELOPMENT

DESCRIPTION: DEVELOP CLAIMS SYSTEM

Pers No.	Name	Grade	Salary scale	Project date joined	Project alloc time
2146	Jones	A1	9	1/3/83	24
3145	Smith	A2	4	2/4/83	24
6126	Black	A1	9	3/4/83	18
1214	Brown	A2	4	4/3/83	18
8191	Green	A1	9	1/5/83	12
7206	Jones	A3	4	1/6/83	7
9137	Brown	A2	4	3/6/83	19

Figure 5.3 Project staff allocation form.

The same question must be posed for the next field. Given the value of project-code (p1) is there only one value of project-location. The answer again is yes – p1 is in London, p4 in Leeds and p5 in Cambridge.

However, the next field fails this test. Given the value of the project-code (p1) there are three possible values of machine-code (m5, m7, m12). This is a repeating group and it must be split up to form its own relation. This is achieved by forming a new relation with the key machine-code (the first data item of the repeating group)

Project-code	Milestone	Date	Supervisor	Machine-code	Empl-code
p1	excavations	28/1/88	2146	m5	3271
"	foundations	2/2/88	"	m5	6191
"	tower	20/2/88	"	m7	3170
"	"	"	"	m12	6191
"	"	"	"	m14	1471
p2	excavations	3/2/88	3145	m5	3271
"	"	"	"	m7	6101
"	tower	5/3/88	"	m14	6191
p3	excavations	4/3/88	2146	m5	3271
p4	excavations	6/3/88	2146	m5	3271

Figure 5.4 Project milestone report.

and project-code (to link it back to the higher group – the form is concerned with machines within a project). This composite key (project-code, machine-code) now becomes the basis of the test on the next attribute. Given a value of project-code (p1) and machine-code (m5) is there only one value of machine-type? The answer is yes (dumper). Notice that we are not considering functional dependency between the key attribute and the non-key data item – this is examined in the next two stages – we are only concerned with ensuring that there is only one value of each non-key item for each value or values of the key field.

The same question is asked for the remaining data items on the form. Given the value of project-code and machine-code (p1, m5) is there only one value of machine-cost, date-required and duration. In each case the answer is yes (200, 21/1/88, 15).

Hence in this example the application of First Normal Form has split the data items into two relations:

Project-code
Project-description
Project-location

Project-code
Machine-code
Machine-type
Machine-cost
Date-required
Duration

First Normal Form effectively splits 'header' and 'line' data. Any number of machines can now be allocated to a particular project.

Second Normal Form is concerned with examining the functional dependency between the key attributes and non-key data items. It identifies part-key dependencies and split these out into new relations. These dependencies are found by posing the question:

Does the value of a non-key data item depend upon the value of (in this example) both values of the key or only one of them?

This question is obviously irrelevant to relations that only have one data item in the key and so this set may proceed to Third Normal Form.

However, we need to consider the relation where project-code and machine-code form the composite key.

Considering each data item in turn; does the value of machine-type (dumper) depend upon project-code (p1) alone, machine-code (m5) alone or both (p1,m5)? The answer appears to be machine-code alone. It does not depend upon project-code alone because p1 produces two values of machine-type (dumper, crane). Similarly, the machine-code appears to be independent of the project-code, p1, m7 and p4, m7 both give the value dumper. In common sense terms the code is stencilled on the side of the physical machine. This machine remains a dumper as it moves from project to project.

The same question is asked of the remaining non-key data items. The following is observed:

- Machine-cost depends upon machine-code alone.
- Date-required depends upon both machine-code and project-code. It cannot depend upon project-code alone (p1 has three date-required values) or machine-code (m7 has three date-required values).
- Duration also depends upon both machine-code and project-code.

Thus at the end of Second Normal Form we now have three relations:

Project-code
Project-description
Project-location

Project-code
Machine-code
Date-required
Duration

Machine-code
Machine-type
Machine-cost

One of the requirements of RDA is that the key of a relation should not contain null values. This means that in the original formulation of the relation with project-code and machine-code as the key, the details of a particular machine could not be stored until it was allocated to a project. This problem is resolved in the Second Normal Form relations. Similarly, the First Normal Form relations meant that if a particular project was deleted and this was the only project that used a certain machine, then details of the machine would also be lost.

Third Normal Form considers inter-non-key dependencies and splits these out to form new relations. These dependencies are found by asking the question:

Is the value of a non-key data item determined by the value of another non-key data item?

For example, in the first group does project-description determine project-location or vice versa. So, are all hospitals built in London and Leeds only has car-park projects?

Some common-sense must be applied here. The company may currently only have one project in Leeds, but to assume a functional dependency would be both absurd and limiting. The same issues arise from the second group. Does date-required (21/1/88) determine duration (15), so all machines hired on that date must be for 15 days? Similarly, we would not wish to build a system where the duration (4 days) determines the hire date (25/1/88).

However, because this is a carefully contrived example to show all three normal forms, there is a functional dependency in the final group. Machine-type (dumper) determines machine-cost (200). This dependency is split out into a new relation.

Machine-type
Machine-cost

However, to retain a link back to the group this was split out from we also leave this new key in the original group:

Machine-code
Machine-type

A failure to maintain this link would lead to information loss – we would not know that m5 was a dumper. This field is marked as a foreign key in the machine-code relation.

Thus after Third Normal Form we are left with four relations that can be named using appropriate singular nouns.

PROJECT
Project-code
Project-description
Project-location

PROJECT MACHINE
Project-code
Machine-code
Date-required
Duration

MACHINE
Machine-code
*Machine-type

MACHINE TYPE
Machine-type
Machine-cost

Third Normal Form has also added improvements to the relations. There are 2,000 dumpers currently used by the company, each with a unique machine-code. If the machine-cost of £200 per day is changed then 2,000 records would have to be altered if the relations were implemented in Second Normal Form. However, in Third Normal Form only one value would need to be changed. Space savings would also result from the creation of this new MACHINE TYPE relation.

The progressive normalization of the data can be documented on formal working papers and these are given in figures 5.5 and 5.6 for Machine Requirements List and the Project Staff Allocation Form. Both of these examples display the three stages of normalization. However, the third form Project Milestone Report demonstrates three further issues.

- **More than one repeating group**. The first repeating group is formed out of project-code and milestone. The second repeating group is formed because project-code (p1) and milestone (tower) does not give one value of machine-code (m7, m12, m13). Consequently a further relation is defined with machine-code as the key and project-code and milestone posted down from the higher group.
- **The order of data items is irrelevant**. This mechanistic approach to normalization should lead to the 'correct' result even if the data items are in an illogical order. Project-code determines supervisor. This might appear obvious and many delegates on our courses list this under First Normal Form. However, following the mechanistic procedure it appears in Second Normal Form after the consideration of the part-key dependencies in the project-code, milestone group.
- **Forms, reports and screens may not pass through all three normal forms**. In this example the analysis is complete at Second Normal Form. All relations pass on unaltered to Third Normal Form. Similarly, forms may not have any repeating groups and indeed may pass directly from UNF to TNF.

The final stage in the normalization procedure is to rationalize the results of the individual forms and bring them into one consolidated group. Relations with the same key are usually merged (as in PROJECT below) and the opportunity is taken to make sure that data names are consistent (empl-code of the Project Milestone Report is re-named pers-no).

Consolidated relations for the project example are:

PROJECT
Project-code
Project-description
Project-location
Project-type
Supervisor

PROJECT MACHINE
Project-code
Machine-code
Date-required
Duration

UNF	FNF	SNF	TNF	Relation-name
Project-code	**Project-code**	**Project-code**	**Project-code**	
Project-description	Project-description	Project-description	Project-description	PROJECT
Project-location	Project-location	Project-location	Project-location	
Machine-code	**Project-code**	**Project-code**	**Project-code**	
Machine-type	**Machine-code**	Machine-code	Machine-code	PROJECT
Machine-cost	Machine-type	Date-required	Date-required	MACHINE
Date-required	Machine-cost	Duration	Duration	
Duration	Date-required	**Machine-code**	**Machine-code**	MACHINE
	Duration	Machine-type	*Machine-type	
		Machine-cost	**Machine-type**	MACHINE
			Machine-cost	TYPE

Figure 5.5 Normalization working paper: machine requirements list.

UNF	FNF	SNF	TNF	Relation-name
Project-code	**Project-code**	**Project-code**	**Project-code**	
Project-type	Project-type	Project-type	Project-type	PROJECT
Project-description	Project-description	Project-description	Project-description	
Pers-No	**Project-code**	**Project-code**	**Project-code**	
Name	**Pers-no**	**Pers-no**	**Pers-no**	PROJECT
Grade	Name	Project-date-join	Project-date-join	PERSON
Salary scale	Grade	Project-alloc-time	Project-alloc-time	
Project-date-join	Salary scale	**Pers-no**	**Pers-no**	EMPLOYEE
Project-alloc-time	Project-date-join	Name	Name	
	Project-alloc-time	Grade	*Grade	
		Salary scale	**Grade**	GRADE
			Salary scale	

Figure 5.6 Normalization working paper: project staff allocation form.

UNF	FNF	SNF	TNF	Relation-name
Project-code	**Project-code**	**Project-code**	**Project-code**	PROJECT
Milestone	**Milestone**	**Milestone**	**Milestone**	MILESTONE
Milestone-date	Milestone-date	Milestone-date	Milestone-date	
Supervisor	Supervisor	**Project-code**	**Project-code**	
Machine-code	**Project-code**	**Milestone**	**Milestone**	ALLOCATION
Empl-code	**Milestone**	**Machine-code**	**Machine-code**	
	Machine-code	Empl-code	Empl-code	
	Empl-code	**Project-code**	**Project-code**	PROJECT
		Supervisor	Supervisor	

Figure 5.7 Normalization working paper: project milestone report.

MACHINE
Machine-code
*Machine-type

MACHINE TYPE
Machine-type
Machine-cost

EMPLOYEE
Pers-no
Name
*Grade

GRADE
Grade
Salary-scale

PROJECT PERSON
Project-code
Pers-no
Project-date-joined
Project-alloc-time

PROJECT MILESTONE
Project-code
Milestone
Milestone-date

ALLOCATION
Project-code
Milestone
Machine-code
Pers-no

Three forms from the Solar Electrical system are analysed in figures 5.8, 5.9 and 5.10. These are used to show further issues that might arise in normalizing documents.

The normalization of the Order Form (figure 5.8) raises the issue of derivable attributes. The line-value may be derived from unit-price and order-quantity. However, only if a complete history of unit prices (and VAT rates) is retained in the data can the line total be derivable at any time. It may be prudent to keep such derived items in the relations until physical design decisions are made. In contrast, the order-total is derivable directly from the line-values and is only given on the Order Form for the convenience of the user. As long as line-values are kept (or are derivable) there is no need to store order-total in the ORDER relation. This form also indicates how indicators, signatures and similar physical attributes of the document are not included in the analysis.

The normalization of the Despatch Note (figure 5.9) is correct but the mechanistic procedure has left a problem that must be resolved during the rationalization process. Customer-no and order-no have both been identified during Third Normal Form and

015440

Solar Electrical

Starlight Road, Wellingborough, Northants NN8 7YH
Telephone: 0933 444222, Fax: 0933 222444

ORDER FORM

CUSTOMER NUMBER   143

CUSTOMER NAME   VFM Electrical supplies

CUSTOMER ADDRESS   32 Victoria Street

                      Nottingham   NG1 3PL

DATE   02/11/96

PRODUCT	PRODUCT DESCRIPTION	UNIT PRICE	QUANTITY	VALUE
11110	Sanyo EM1614 M/wave	123.25	2	246.50
10209	Zanussi DR56L fridge	152.00	4	608.00
			ORDER TOTAL	854.50

FOR OFFICE USE ONLY

CREDIT CLEARANCE ☑   Signature _G.K. Panman_

UNF	FNF	SNF	TNF	Relation-name
Order-no	**Order-no**	**Order-no**	**Order-no**	
Cust-no	Cust-no	Cust-No	*Cust-No	ORDER
Cust-name	Cust-name	Cust-name	Order-date	
Cust-address	Cust-address	Cust-address	Order-total	
Order-date	Order-date	Order-date	**Order-no**	
Prod-code	**Order-no**	Order-total	**Prod-code**	ORDER LINE
Prod-description	**Prod-code**	**Order-no**	Order-qty	
Unit-price	Prod-description	**Prod-code**	Line-value	
Order-qty	Unit-price	Order-qty	**Prod-code**	
Line-value	Order-qty	Line-value	Prod-description	PRODUCT
Order-total	Line-value	**Prod-code**	Unit-price	
	Order-total	Prod-description	**Cust-no**	
		Unit-price	Cust-name	CUSTOMER
			Cust-address	

Figure 5.8 Normalization working paper: order form.

Solar Electrical

Starlight Road, Wellingborough, Northants NN8 7YH
Telephone: 0933 444222, Fax: 0933 222444

DESPATCH NOTE *No: 815172*

Customer Number	15 Date: 20/08/9φ
Customer Name	VALUE VISION
Customer Address	14 CHEQUERS WAY
	SUTTON COLDFIELD
Order Number:	321-7628-X Order Date: 17/08/9φ

DELIVERY INSTRUCTIONS: Closed 1200-13.00

DELIVERY DATE: 21/08/9φ

Product	Product Description	Quantity
01816	Multiman	3φ
04908	JVC 14" TV (remote)	17
02176	Camcorder -02	5

Drivers Signature _Jerry_   Customers Signature

Copy   1. DESPATCH (white)   2. CUSTOMER (yellow)   3. ACCOUNTS (blue)

UNF	FNF	SNF	TNF	Relation-name
Desp-note-no	**Desp-note-no**	**Desp-note-no**	**Desp-note-no**	
Cust-no	Cust-no	Cust-no	*Cust-No	DESPATCH
Desp-note-date	Desp-note-date	Desp-note-date	Desp-note-date	
Cust-name	Cust-name	Cust-name	*Order-no	
Cust-address	Cust-address	Cust-address	Del-instructions	
Order-no	Order-no	Order-no	Del-date	
Order-date	Order-date	Order-date	**Cust-no**	
Del-instructions	Del-instructions	Del-instructions	Cust-name	CUSTOMER
Del-date	Del-date	Del-date	Cust-address	
Prod-code	**Desp-note-no**	**Desp-note-no**	**Order-no**	ORDER
Prod-description	**Prod-code**	**Prod-code**	Order-date	
Desp-qty	Prod-description	Desp-qty	**Desp-note-no**	DESPATCH LINE
	Desp-qty	**Prod-code**	**Prod-code**	
		Prod-description	Desp-qty	
			Prod-code	PRODUCT
			Prod-description	

Figure 5.9 Normalization working paper: despatch note.

SOLAR ELECTRICAL PRODUCTS

REGIONAL SALES REPORT

REGION NUMBER: 4

REGION MIDLANDS

Customer No	Customer name	Orders YTD	Value orders YTD
15	Value Vision	20	14,240
48	Derby Electrical Supplies	15	8,431
49	Anypart Electrical	28	9,898
103	Leicester Appliances	10	6,040
▪	▪	▪	▪
▪	▪	▪	▪
▪	▪	▪	▪
▪	▪	▪	▪
▪	▪	▪	▪
▪	▪	▪	▪
▪	▪	▪	▪
392	Solar, Nottingham	30	25,785
Totals		300	120000

UNF	FNF	SNF	TNF	Relation-name
Region-no	**Region-no**	**Region-no**	**Region-no**	REGION
Region-description	Region-description	Region-description	Region-description	
Customer-no	**Region-no**	**Region-no**		
Customer-name	**Customer-no**	**Customer-no**	**Customer-no**	
Orders-YTD	Customer-name		Customer-name	
	Orders-YTD	**Customer-no**	Orders-YTD	CUSTOMER
		Customer-name	*Region-no	
		Orders-YTD		

Figure 5.10 Normalization working paper: regional sales report.

marked as foreign keys. However, there is a dependency between these two data items. Each value of order-no will only give one value of customer-no. Hence the rationalization process should also look for unwanted dependency between foreign keys.

Finally, the order of data items in the normalization of the Customer Sales Report has led to an all key group Customer-no and Region-no (figure 5.10). However, because all customer numbers are unique, customer-no determines region-no. This has been resolved in Third Normal Form so demonstrating that this test should also be applied to *inter-key* dependencies as well as inter non-key data items.

5.4 Logical data model

A Logical Data Model can be created from the set of normalized relations. The following steps are applied.

- Create an entity type for each relation.
- Relations with composite keys are made the detail (or many) end of a one to many (1:m) relationship with the relations where one of the attributes is the sole primary key. For example, the entity PROJECT MACHINE with the composite key project-code, machine-code is made a detail (or many end) of a 1:many relationship with the entities where each item is a primary key, i.e. PROJECT (project-code) and MACHINE (machine-code). The same applies to PROJECT PERSON and to PROJECT MILESTONE. The latter example does not have an owner entity for milestone. The rules state that one must be created (MILESTONE TYPE) with milestone as the key.

  It can now be seen that these composite key entities are actually intersection entities needed to resolve many-to-many relationships and that this was the main purpose of First Normal Form. Figure 5.11 shows the application of the first two steps.

- A relation with a foreign key is made the detail of the relation that has the foreign key as its complete primary key. Hence MACHINE, with the foreign key of machine-type, is made the many end of a 1:many relationship with the relation MACHINE TYPE where machine-type is the complete primary key. EMPLOYEE has grade as a foreign key and hence is linked to the GRADE relation. It is useful at this stage to review whether the key of new relations formed by the second step (e.g. MILESTONE TYPE) appear as attributes somewhere and hence must now be marked as foreign keys and relationships established.

- Compound keys (here defined as relations with more than two data items in the key) are also made details of relations where each data item appears as the complete primary key *unless* there is a relation where a group of the items already appear together in a key. This is best explained by example. ALLOCATION has the triple key project-code, milestone and machine-code. At first glance this should be related to the three entities PROJECT (project-code), MACHINE (machine-code) and MILESTONE TYPE (milestone) in three one-to-many relationships. However project-code and milestone are already related in PROJECT MILESTONE (project-code, milestone) and project-code and machine-code in PROJECT MACHINE. Hence ALLOCATION is related to these two entities and not the three separate ones. In common sense terms values of ALLOCATION can only be formed for valid combinations of project-code and milestone and project-code and machine-code.

  The rules are summarized in figure 5.12.

- Relationships are named and optionality indicated. Compound and composite keys always have mandatory relationships with their master entities. However foreign keys that are not part of the identifier may have null values and hence have an optional relationship with the master entity. The naming conventions may be applied at this time and this may identify new relationships. For example supervisor in PROJECT is actually a pers-no field that plays the role of supervisor. This role can now be moved to the relationship name and pers-no included in PROJECT relation as a foreign key.

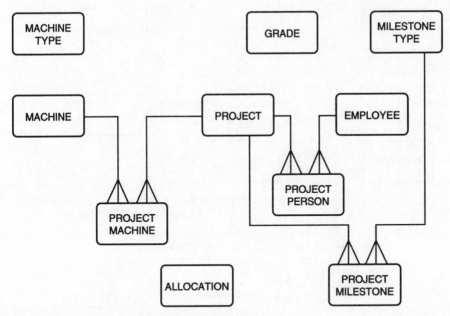

Figure 5.11 Logical data structure (Steps 1 and 2).

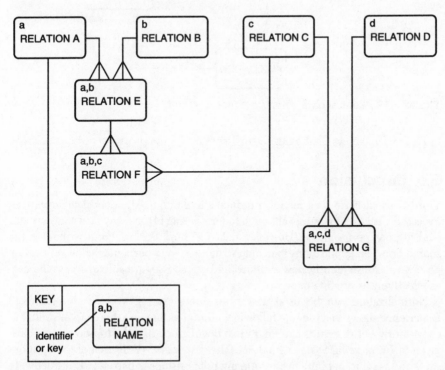

Figure 5.12 Rules for forming relationships.

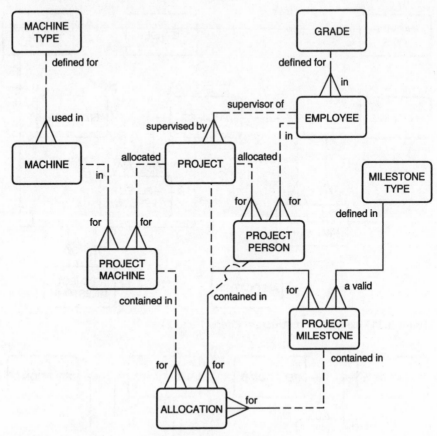

Figure 5.13 Logical data structure (Steps 3, 4 and 5).

Figure 5.13 shows the Logical Data Structure for the project reporting example.

5.5 Conclusion

Third Normal Form data models produce simple non-redundant data structures. Processing is logically simple although the traversing of too many data relations may lead to poor performance. However, data in Third Normal Form is more easily shared between applications than data structured for a particular set of application processes. Consequently, new applications or processes are able to access the data as effectively as existing ones.

Normalization can be used at various times during systems development. Experience shows that the rule following method outlined in this chapter produces consistently better results among trainee developers than the top-down approach given in *Introducing Systems Analysis*. The 'automatic' derivation of the relationships and resolution of the many-to-many relationships is particularly attractive to delegates coming to formal data design for the first time.

6 Logical Process Design

6.1 Introduction

The accurate and unambiguous specification of processes is at the heart of systems design. Specifications must be presented in such a way that users can confidently sign off the process designs that describe how their system will work. This demands models that are accessible to users but are sufficiently precise that the chance of mis-interpretation is minimized.

Most designers are aware of the problems of 'mis-understandings' and the problems, negotiations and re-criminations that arise from differences of interpretation. Many deal with this uncertainty by specifying processes in painstaking programming detail – often down to which file to find a field in and where to store the results of a calculation. Unfortunately this detail has two unwanted results. Firstly, the users are unable to sign off the specification because the business process (which they understand) is buried in the middle of programs, file layouts and field names (which they don't). Developers often cope with this by writing a second specification (often called the business specification) in a language the users understands. Unfortunately this language is usually narrative ambiguous English with an unpredictable consistency with the 'tight' process specification given to the programmer. Secondly, the painstaking specification serves to reduce the work interest of the programmers who begin to see themselves as unmotivated 'coding monkeys'.

Developers need to understand the business process but the individual specification does not need to tell them how to program it. Standard programming guidelines and Interface Style Guides will do this. Many specifications unnecessarily repeat standards, interface guidelines and Data Dictionary definitions that are common to all developments. Furthermore, the process specification should be independent of the programming language and formulated in such a way that it promotes re-usability and modularity.

Methodologies find it difficult to agree on process specification. This chapter looks at two approaches in detail. The first is Action Diagramming. In this book it is used in conjunction with the Data Flow Diagram, but it can stand alone as a method for specifying processes in legacy systems where no system documentation exists. The second method is the Update Process Model of SSADM Version 4. The attraction of this approach is that it offers an object-oriented perspective of the system (through the extended Entity Life History) before reorganizing it to produce a more conventional view.

Enquiry-only processes are briefly considered in the Logical Access Map (LAM) and the Enquiry Access Path (EAP). Less space is given to this less demanding area of systems design.

6.2 Structured English

Data Flow Diagrams depict the processes that will become programs, procedures and protocols in the required system. The details of each process must be defined to provide an unambiguous process (or program) specification.

An Action Diagram is defined for each bottom level process of the Data Flow Diagram. This describes the logic of the process and Stepwise Refinement can then be applied to produce detailed program definitions.

Action Diagrams and Stepwise Refinement are both based on Structured English. Structured English is a method of specifying unambiguous narrative. It contains three basic constructs:

- sequence;
- selection;
- iteration.

Indentation is used to show dependency.

Sequence

Sequences of events or actions are described by the top to bottom order of the statements.

Example

DO admission procedure
Accept application
Store applicant data
Add to list of applicants
Send letter of acknowledgement
ENDDO

Selection

Actions are often dependent upon current conditions. The selection of the appropriate action is defined using either an IF...ELSE...ENDIF or a CASE... OTHERWISE...ENDCASE construct.

IF statements may be simple, exclusive, compound or nested.

Examples

Simple IF

```
IF type 'A' customer
   apply discount to total-price
ENDIF
```

Exclusive IF

```
IF type 'A' customer
   apply type-A-discount to total-price
ELSE (type B customer)
   apply type-B-discount to total-price
ENDIF
```

Compound IF

```
IF type 'A' customer OR order-value >= discount-level
   apply type-A-discount to total-price
ELSE (type 'B' customer AND value < discount-level)
   apply type-B-discount to total-price
ENDIF
```

Nested IF

```
IF type 'A' customer
   apply type-A-discount to total-price
ELSE (not type 'A' customer)
   IF type 'B' customer
      apply type-B-discount to total-price
   ELSE (not type 'B' customer)
      IF type 'C' customer
         apply type-C-discount to total-price
      ELSE (not type 'C' customer)
         apply standard-discount to total-price
      ENDIF
   ENDIF
ENDIF
```

CASE constructs are used where one of a number of exclusive options will be selected. OTHERWISE may be used as a 'catch-all' construct.

DOCASE

Example

```
DO CASE
CASE type 'A' customer
   apply type-A-discount to total-price
CASE type 'B' customer
   apply type-B-discount to total-price
CASE type 'C' customer
   apply type-C-discount to total-price
CASE type 'D' customer
   apply type-D-discount to total-price
OTHERWISE
   apply standard-discount to total-price
ENDCASE
```

Repetition

Repetition is defined using one of three Structured English statements, DO WHILE...ENDDO, DO...UNTIL or FOR ALL...ENDFOR. DOWHILE and DO...UNTIL evaluate conditions. DO WHILE evaluates the condition before any action is taken, DO...UNTIL evaluates the condition after.

Examples

```
DO WHILE orders exist
   :
   : Process order statements
   :
ENDDO
```

If no order exists then the process order statements will never be actioned.

```
DO
   :
   : Process order statements
   :
UNTIL no more orders
```

The process order statements will be performed at least once. This process definition assumes the presence of a least one order.

Most programming languages directly support Structured English constructs and the Structured English verbs may be tailored to match the in-house standard language as long as the structure is retained:

Example

    PERFORM
      :
      : Process order statements
      :
    UNTIL no more orders

This example uses the PERFORM verb (COBOL) in place of DO. The unambiguous structure of the original construct is preserved.

Stepwise Refinement is a 'top-down' technique used to decompose complex processes into manageable sub-functions. This technique extends the approach introduced at the higher level in Data Flow Diagramming.

At the highest level, the Structured English may define a process without attention to detail. The detail is assumed to be contained in a sub-function. Sub-functions are identified in capitals and are the object of DO verbs.

Example

    DO CREATE SALES ORDER
      :
      DO WHILE orders exist
        DO APPLY DISCOUNT
        DO ALLOCATE STOCK
      ENDDO
      DO PRODUCE ORDER-ERROR-REPORT
    ENDDO

The detailed processing involved in APPLY DISCOUNT, ALLOCATE STOCK and PRODUCE ORDER-ERROR-REPORT will be defined separately as in:

Example

    DO APPLY DISCOUNT
      DO CASE
      CASE type 'A' customer
        apply type-A-discount to total-price
      CASE type 'B' customer
        apply type-B-discount to total-price
      CASE type 'C' customer
        apply type-C-discount to total-price
      CASE type 'D' customer
        apply type-D-discount to total-price
      OTHERWISE
        apply standard-discount to total-price
      ENDCASE
    END DO

```
DO ALLOCATE STOCK
   DO lines (on order)
      IF line-item is valid stock item
         decrement item-stock-level by line-item-qty
         flag line-item as allocated
      ELSE (not valid stock item)
         DO CREATE ORDER-ERROR LINE
      ENDIF
   UNTIL no more order lines
END DO
```

6.3 Action Diagrams

The Structured English modules are now extended to create action diagrams. This enforces a review of the process definitions and improves the readability of the model. Action Diagrams use brackets to connect the decision points in the Structured English constructs and to emphasize the dependencies shown by indentation.

Example

```
┌─ DO APPLY DISCOUNT
│  ┌─ DO CASE
│  ├─ CASE type 'A' customer
│        apply type-A-discount to total-price
│  ├─ CASE type 'B' customer
│        apply type-B-discount to total-price
│  ├─ CASE type 'C' customer
│        apply type-C-discount to total-price
│  ├─ CASE type 'D' customer
│        apply type-D-discount to total-price
│  ├─ OTHERWISE
│        apply standard-discount to total-price
│  └─ ENDCASE
└─ ENDDO
```

Repetition blocks are denoted with a double line at the decision point.

Examples

```
╔═ DO WHILE orders exist
║  :
║  : Process order statements
║  :
╚─ ENDDO
```

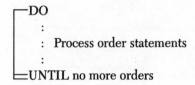

┌─DO
│   ⋮
│   ⋮ Process order statements
│   ⋮
└═UNTIL no more orders

Exit-points may be added to the diagram. An arrowed line points to the level that will be active after the exit.

Examples

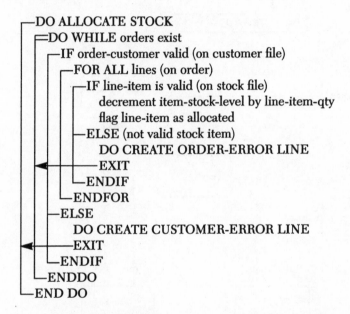

┌─DO ALLOCATE STOCK
│ ┌═DO WHILE orders exist
│ │ ┌─IF order-customer valid (on customer file)
│ │ │ ┌─FOR ALL lines (on order)
│ │ │ │ ┌─IF line-item is valid (on stock file)
│ │ │ │ │   decrement item-stock-level by line-item-qty
│ │ │ │ │   flag line-item as allocated
│ │ │ │ ├─ELSE (not valid stock item)
│ │ │ │ │   DO CREATE ORDER-ERROR LINE
◄─┤ │ │ │ ├──EXIT
│ │ │ │ └─ENDIF
│ │ │ └─ENDFOR
│ │ ├─ELSE
│ │ │   DO CREATE CUSTOMER-ERROR LINE
◄─┤ │ ├──EXIT
│ │ └─ENDIF
│ └─ENDDO
└─END DO

If a stock item is invalid, that order is discarded and the next order is processed. If the customer is invalid, the process defines an exit from the routine. Note that the exit statements are only necessary where the natural order of processing is not applicable. That is, if the EXIT statements were not present, an invalid stock item line would be discarded and the next line on the order would be processed. Likewise, if a customer were invalid, the next order would be processed.

6.4 Extended action diagramming conventions (ADAPT)

We have extended the Action Diagram to include elements of the dialogue as well as cross-references to the entities of the Logical Data Structure. Figure 6.1 shows a fragment of a Data Flow Diagram and a Logical Data Structure for an order processing system. The relevant parts of the entity descriptions are as follows:

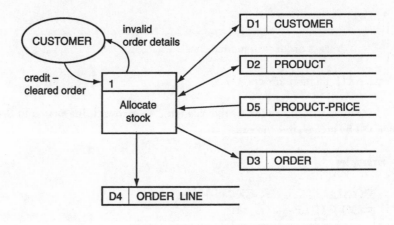

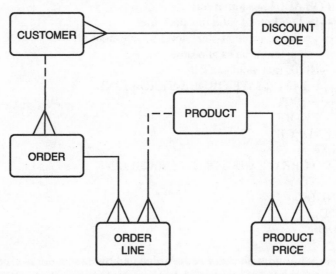

Figure 6.1 (a) Fragment of the data flow diagram and (b) Fragment of the logical data structure.

CUSTOMER
Customer-no
Customer-name
Customer-address
Orders-year-to-date
*Discount-code

PRODUCT
Product-no
Product-description

PRODUCT-PRICE
Product-no
Discount-code
Discount-price

ORDER
Order-no
Order-date
*Customer-no

ORDER LINE
Order-no
Product-no
Order-qty

DISCOUNT CODE
Discount-code
Discount-code description

Figure 6.2 shows that Action Diagram for the process Allocate Stock.
The Action Diagram includes notation to show:

- **Existence checks.** This is to check that the entered value exists in the entity occurrences for that entity type. The ADAPT interface rules define how to cope with the failure of an existence check. It is not necessary to define these rules in every business process specification.
- **Mandatory fields.** These are emboldened.
- **Entity cross-references.** Entities are shown in brackets, e.g. [ENTITY]. These references should tally with the Reads and Writes of the Data Flow Diagram.

However, no attempt is made to show value and format checks. ADAPT defines these within the Data Dictionary.

Within ADAPT a number of reserved words are used to denote certain types of operation. For example, Confirm presents a default value that can be over-written.

Action Diagrams are also used to control the decomposition of Data Flow Diagrams. In ADAPT a process does not have to be reduced any further if it is possible to write the process description on a side of A4 using the standard action diagramming convention demonstrated in figure 6.2.

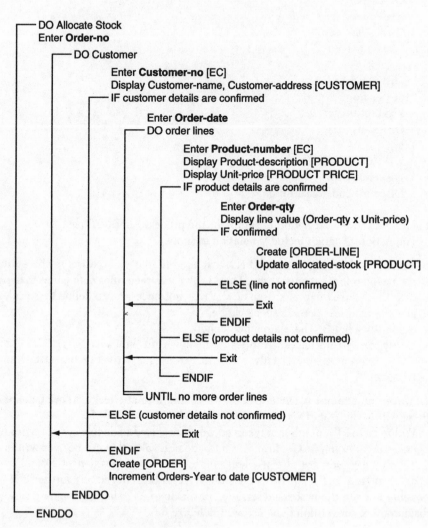

Figure 6.2 Action diagram: allocate stock.

6.5 SSADM Version 4: update process specification

6.5.1 Entity Life History: operations

Operations are discrete components of processing in each effect box of the Entity Life History. The major operations are as follows:

- **Store the initial key value – the birth effect.** For example, Store Region-no.
- **Store initial attribute values – birth effect.** For example, Store region-description.
- **Store an attribute value using an expression – birth effect.** For example, Store Orders-year-to-date = 0
- **Store an attribute value – mid-life effect.** For example, the value of the data item despatch-date is not known when the order is created – hence, it is left blank during the creation of the initial attributes of order. However, once the despatch note is raised then the despatch date can be posted into the order entity hence storing an attribute value in the order entity's mid-life. This may again be qualified with an expression.
- **Replace an attribute using an expression – mid-life effect.** For example, Replace Orders-year-to-date with Orders-year-to-date + 1 or Replace Order-value-year-to-date with Order-value-year-to-date + order-value.
- SSADM also allows cut and tie operations to make relationships between detail and master entities. In our examples we have replaced these with storing and deleting values of the foreign key. For example, storing discount-code in the Customer entity effectively ties an occurrence of Customer to a valid Discount Code.

Furthermore, SSADM permits practitioners to add additional types of operations that they feel might be useful. For example, we have used:

- **Increment an attribute value.** For example, increment orders-year-to-date might be preferable to the rather ungainly Replace orders-year-to-date with orders-year-to-date + 1.

The operations being considered are still logical, physical types of operations such as reading before modifying, sorting and error handling are not included.

The operations are listed on the ELH and given a number. These numbers are shown on the diagram in small boxes attached beneath the effect to which they relate.

Figure 6.3 shows a partial entity/event grid for the order processing system introduced in figure 6.1. The extended entity and attribute set is listed below:

CUSTOMER
Customer-no
Customer-name
Customer-address
Orders-year-to-date
Order-value-year-to-date
*Discount-code

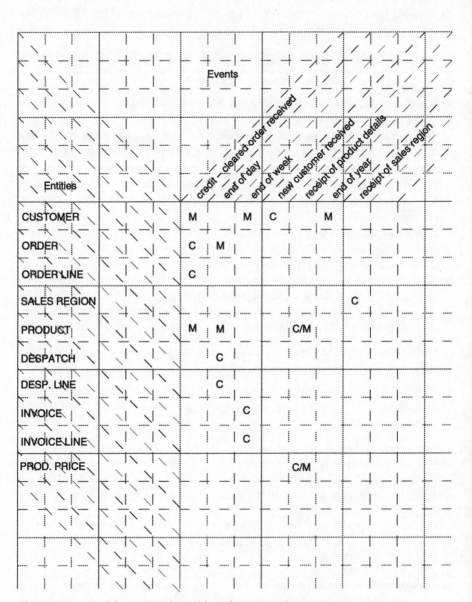

Figure 6.3   Partial event/entity grid: order processing system.

PRODUCT
Product-no
Product-description
allocated-stock
physical-stock

PRODUCT-PRICE
Product-no
Discount-code
Discount-price

ORDER
Order-no
Order-date
*Customer-no
Despatch-date

ORDER LINE
Order-no
Product-no
Order-qty

DISCOUNT CODE
Discount-code
Discount-code-description

Figures 6.4 to 6.7 show the initial Entity Life Histories for Customer, Order, Order Line and Product.

6.5.2 State Indicators

State Indicators are a method of controlling the sequencing of events. They may be thought of as an additional attribute within each entity. Each time an event affects an entity occurrence the state indicator is updated to indicate that the particular effect has occurred. Holding a state indicator in each entity means that it is possible to detect the state that a particular entity occurrence has reached in its life. Knowing the current state of an entity occurrence means that it is possible to determine whether it is valid to apply the effect of a particular event to that entity occurrence.

The notation for state indicators is as follows:

Valid prior value(s)/Set to value

The valid prior value(s) are the values of the state indicator that must exist for the effect of an event to take place. There may be many of these values and they may

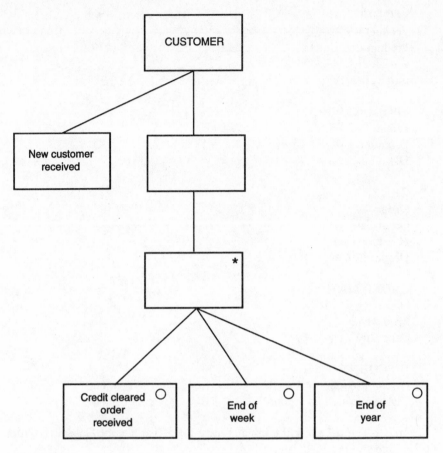

Figure 6.4 Customer: initial entity life history.

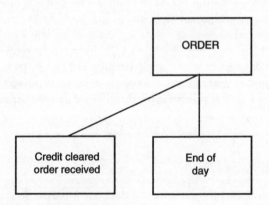

Figure 6.5 Order: initial entity life history.

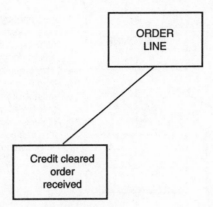

Figure 6.6 Order line: initial entity life history.

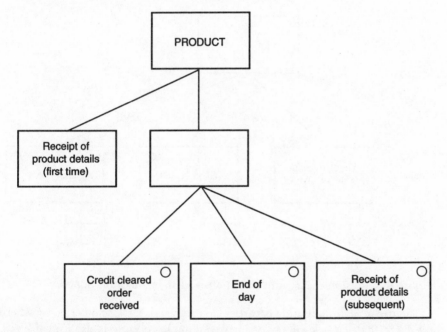

Figure 6.7 Product: initial entity life history.

include the Set to value of that event. For example, in the ELH for Customer (figure 6.8), the receipt of a credit cleared order, setting the State Indicator (SI) to 2, may be followed by another credit cleared order. Hence 2 is also a valid prior value of the State Indicator for this event.

The Set to value is the value given to the SI once the effect of the event has been completed. There will only be one set to value for each event within each ELH. The set to SI value of 1 is usually allocated to the birth effect and subsequent effects are numbered sequentially through the diagram.

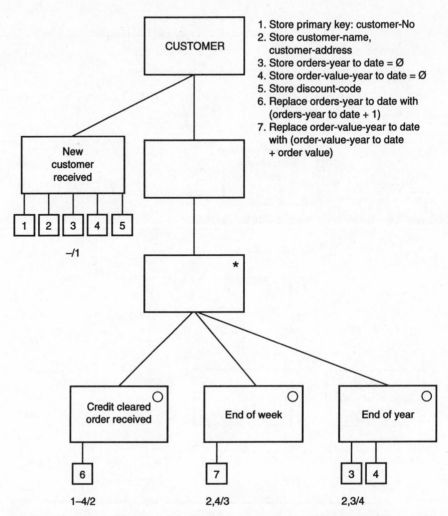

Figure 6.8 Customer ELH with operations and state indicators added.

The use of State Indicators is particularly shown in the Customer entity where the event End of Week will not be invoked if the last event was also End of Week. This means that no orders were placed in that week and that the week did not include an End-of-Year. Consequently, there is no need to raise an invoice for this customer. Thus entity occurrences with an SI of 3 will be unaffected by this event.

The prior value of the birth event and the Set to value of the termination events are both indicated by a null state indicator, a hyphen (-).

Figures 6.8 to 6.11 show the ELHs with operations and State Indicators added.

6.5.3 Effect Correspondence Diagram

An Effect Correspondence Diagram (ECD) is drawn for each event with the name

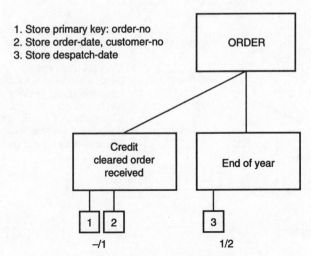

1. Store primary key: order-no
2. Store order-date, customer-no
3. Store despatch-date

Figure 6.9 Order: ELH with operations and state indicators added.

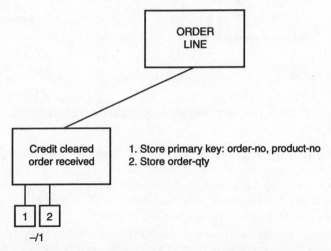

1. Store primary key: order-no, product-no
2. Store order-qty

Figure 6.10 Order line: ELH with operations and state indicators added.

of each event as the heading. It demonstrates how the entities affected by each event are related to each other. The event/entity grid and the Logical Data Structure are important prerequisites for developing the ECD. The event/entity grid will show which entities are affected by a particular event and the Logical Data Structure will record how these particular entities are related to each other. Effects are represented by round-cornered boxes. The following circumstances have to be accommodated by the ECD:

- **Single effect on single entity occurrence.** If an event has a single effect on just one occurrence of an entity then the effect box contains the name of the entity affected by the event.

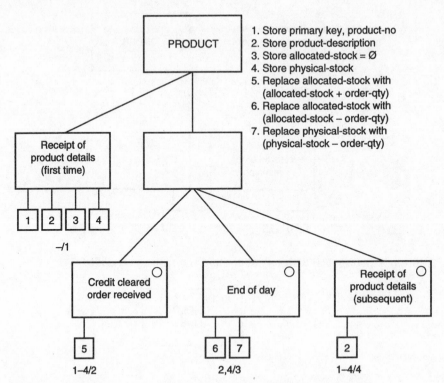

Figure 6.11 Product: ELH with operations and state indicators added.

- **Selection**. The selection notation is used when an event has an effect on a single entity occurrence in two or more mutually exclusive ways.
- **Iteration**. If a single instance of an event causes more than one occurrence of a particular entity to be changed then the iteration of the event on the set of entity occurrences is depicted using the iteration structure.
- **Simultaneous effects**. There are occasions when a single instance of an event affects more than one occurrence of an entity, each occurrence being affected in a different way. This is known as a simultaneous effect.
- **One-to-one correspondence**. The one-to-one correspondence between the effects of a single event is shown by a bi-directional arrow. There will be a one-to-one correspondence when an instance of an event causes one occurrence of an effect on one entity occurrence and also one occurrence of another effect to another entity occurrence. This brings together all the effects associated with one event into a single diagram.

An Effect Correspondence Diagram is developed in the following way:

- **Draw a box representing each Entity affected by the event**. An ECD is developed for each event. The affected entities are identified by looking to see which ELHs include the specified event. This should be obvious from the event/entity grid. The entities affected by the named event are then drawn using 'soft' boxes placed in a similar layout to their positions on the LDS.

■ **Draw separate boxes for simultaneous effects**. A simultaneous effect occurs when an instance of an event may logically affect more than one entity occurrence, each occurrence being affected in a different way. On the ELH this will be shown as the same event name qualified with different roles.

■ **Include mutually exclusive effects**. An event that has two or more mutually exclusive effects on an entity is shown as a selection on the ECD. Mutually exclusive events can be recognized on an ELH as duplicated events qualified by exclusivity.

■ **Add iterations**. Iteration occurs where of an event causes a set of entity occurrences to be updated by the same effect.

■ **Add one-to-one correspondences between effects**. Bi-directional arrows are added to the diagram where an effect on an occurrence of one entity type corresponds to an effect on an occurrence or occurrences of another entity type. One-to-one correspondences occur when one entity is a detail of another, indicating access from detail to master.

■ **Merge iterative effects**. If an entity is affected by an event in more than one iterative way and access to the entity is via the same relationship, then the effects can be merged into a single structure.

■ **Add non-updated entities**. To complete the ECDs it is now necessary to include nodes to represent entities that need to be accessed to traverse the data structure and entities from which data is retrieved but which are not updated.

■ **Add event data**. The entry point is indicated by a single headed arrow against the first entity to be accessed. Associated with the entry point is the event data. These are attributes that are entered into the update process and will normally consist of a key attribute together with any attributes that carry updating information.

The ECD for the event 'Credit cleared order received' is shown in figure 6.12. Notice the iteration of Order Line for Order and the one-to-one correspondence of Order to Customer and Order Line to Product.

6.5.4 Update Process Model

The Update Process Model is developed from the Effect Correspondence Diagram and the Entity Life Histories. The effects that are in one-to-one correspondence on the ECD are grouped together by drawing a box around them. Each of these groups is given a descriptive name (see figure 6.13). The opportunity has also been taken to re-position these entities.

The operations for each entity on the ECD are then copied over from the appropriate nodes of each Entity Life History. This includes the test of the prior State Indicator to detect an error condition and also the Set to State Indicator when the effect is completed. The operations are listed within entity and no attempt is made to show the order of operations within the whole event.

Finally, the operations are placed within the structure in their order of occurrence and conditions are added. An example of this Update Process Model is shown in figure 6.14.

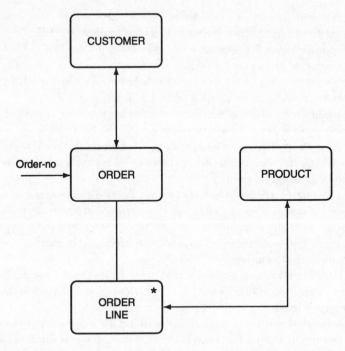

Figure 6.12 Effect correspondence diagram: credit cleared order received.

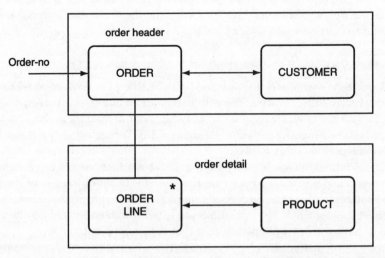

Figure 6.13 Effect correspondence diagram: credit cleared order received with named groups.

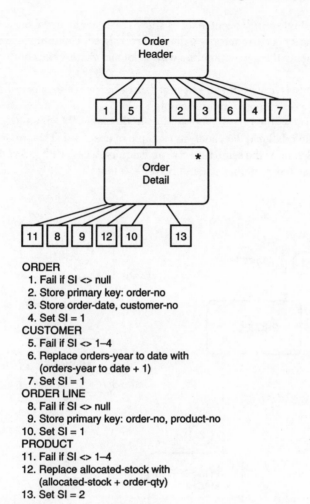

ORDER
1. Fail if SI <> null
2. Store primary key: order-no
3. Store order-date, customer-no
4. Set SI = 1
CUSTOMER
5. Fail if SI <> 1–4
6. Replace orders-year to date with
   (orders-year to date + 1)
7. Set SI = 1
ORDER LINE
8. Fail if SI <> null
9. Store primary key: order-no, product-no
10. Set SI = 1
PRODUCT
11. Fail if SI <> 1–4
12. Replace allocated-stock with
    (allocated-stock + order-qty)
13. Set SI = 2

Figure 6.14 Update process model: credit cleared order received.

6.6 Logical Access Maps

Action Diagrams are used to define processes that change stored data. This corresponds to events explored on the entity/event grid where read-only activities are also omitted because, by definition, an event must change stored data.

However, the way that read-only activities, like reports and enquiries, traverse the data model may be importance. Speed of retrieval and enquiry will be affected by the number of entities that must be accessed.

Major retrievals and reports can be examined in Logical Access Maps (LAMs). This shows the navigation path for each transaction superimposed on the entity model.

The sequence of actions is denoted by a number against the access symbol.

Retrieval of a single entity occurrence is shown by a single arrow head. Access to a number of entity occurrences by a double arrow head. Conditional accesses are shown by breaking the navigation line with a dot and writing the condition alongside.

LAMs will prove very useful for physical data design when the normalized model is flexed to support response requirements.

Figure 6.15 shows the Logical Access Map for the report 'Machine Requirements List' used in the relational data analysis example in chapter 5. The opportunity has also been used to show the same report as an Enquiry Access Path (SSADM Version 4). The notation and principles should be self-evident.

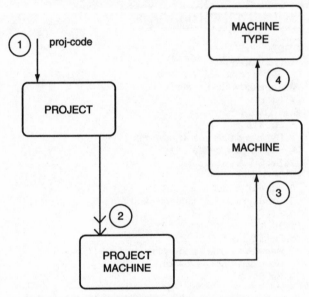

Figure 6.15 Logical access map: machine requirements list.

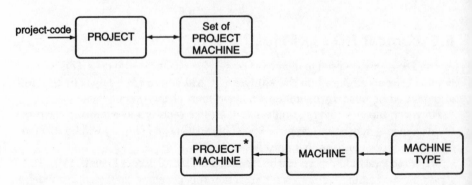

Figure 6.16 Enquiry access path: machine requirements list.

6.7 Conclusion

This chapter has presented two main models for update process definition. Their development is shown graphically in figure 6.17.

Two further models have been developed for enquiry processes. There is little agreement on methods of process or function definition and there are many more candidate diagrams for this area of design and some will be encountered in the chapter on object orientation. However, readers are invited to assess the usefulness of these models against the following criteria and to make their own conclusion. My guess is that you will not find an overall winner. Some methods are strong in one area and weak in others:

1. ease of correct interpretation by the user;
2. ease of correct interpretation by the programmer;

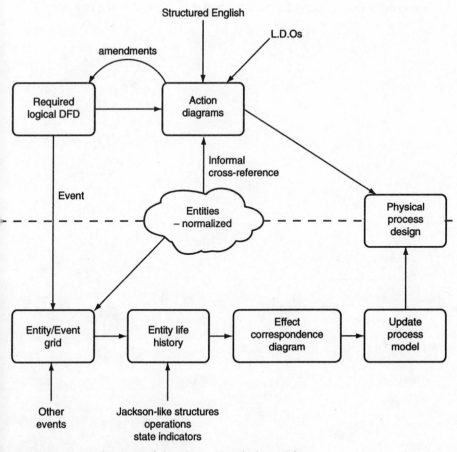

Figure 6.17 A diagram of the alternative design paths.

3. absence of ambiguity;
4. object-orientation: applicability to object-oriented programming languages;
5. promotion of re-usability;
6. application in legacy systems.

My practical perception of the strengths and weaknesses of the Action Diagram and the Update Project Process Model are given below:

Criteria	Action Diagram	Update Process Model
1	Good	Poor
2	Good	Good
3	Good	Excellent
4	Poor	Good
5	Poor	Good
6	Excellent	Poor

A final criteria for assessment – promotion of good programming practice will be considered in chapter 8.

7 Object-oriented Design

7.1 Introduction

Object-oriented analysis (OOA) was introduced in the companion text *Introducing Systems Analysis*. It considered the emergence of generic models and template software as well as introducing Meyer's (1988) notation and constructs and his arguments for an object rather than functional approach to systems development.

In this chapter we review OOA methods before moving on to look at the principles and expression of object-oriented development using a representative notation.

7.2 Object-oriented analysis

In Booch's (1994) review of proven approaches for analysis he identifies a number of mechanisms for discovering classes and objects. The prototyping approach has been considered elsewhere (see chapter 4). However, five further mechanisms are reviewed below:

- **Domain analysis.** This seeks to identify classes and objects that are common to all applications within a given domain. This is essentially the same principle as generic models where key objects, operations and relationships have been identified by 'domain experts'. Analysts undertaking work in unfamiliar business areas may be helped by access to such generic models, subsequently refining them to accommodate particular requirements. The similarity of this to Checkland's soft systems approach has been noted in the companion text.
- **Classical data approaches.** The similarity between entities of conventional data analysis and objects was noted in *Introducing Systems Analysis*. Indeed Coad and Yourdon (1991) suggest that Shlaer and Mellor's book on *Object-oriented Systems Analysis* (1994) might be better titled *Making Semantic Data Modelling Practical*. Booch's own example for Inventory Tracking produces key abstractions that resemble entities.

■ **Behaviour analysis.** This focuses upon behaviour rather than static things. Booch (1994) quotes Rubin and Goldberg: the approach we use emphasises first understanding what takes place in the system. These are the system behaviours. We next assign these behaviours to parts of the system and try to understand who initiates and who participates in these behaviours. This approach is geared towards business function. Diagramming our understanding of the systems (through, for example, Data Flow Diagrams or System Flowcharts) should help us identify objects, classes and relationships.

■ **Use case analysis.** This is essentially the walkthrough of scenarios that are fundamental to the business system. Primary scenarios might be:
 – customer telephones to book a course place;
 – manager requests a monthly sales analysis;
 – invoice is sent to customer requesting payment.

Each of these is walked through in detail. As the walkthrough progresses objects will be identified and responsibilities, properties and effects of each object considered and documented. Booch (1994) suggests that a storyboard is built up. A prototype or Data Flow Diagram are other possibilities.

As development progresses these initial scenarios are extended to consider exceptional conditions as well as secondary or peripheral topics. Examples might include:

■ The course is full.
■ The invoice is only part-paid.

Booch constructs scripted interaction diagrams for these that may also incorporate elements of Structured English.

Structured Analysis is a term used by Booch (1994) to refer to what we call Data Flow Diagrams. His main objection is to models that include an essence of design rather than what he terms the 'essential model'. Current physical DFDs seem reasonable analysis tools to support both use-case and behaviour analysis. Object-oriented writers seem to be concerned that a Data Flow Diagram approach will necessarily lead on to a top-down functional decomposition. However, this does not have to be the case. The Data Flow Diagram may be used as primarily an analysis tool with little contribution to the design task. The design weakness of the DFD has already been noted in chapter 1.

The logical Data Dictionary is still fundamental to the object-oriented approach. It is developed and updated as development progresses.

7.3 Object notation and constructs

Rumbaugh *et al.* (1991) defines an object as a concept, abstraction or 'thing with crisp boundaries and meaning for the problem at hand'. All objects have an identity and are distinguishable. Examples might include:

■ Order number 1257;
■ The Assist Partnership;

■ Martin Pearson;
■ Larry the Lamb.

These object instances are identical to entity occurrences defined elsewhere. However, Booch (1994) demonstrates the difference between an entity occurrence and an object instance by stating that the object has state, identity and behaviour. Hence, any notation we use for expressing object instances (and classes) should allow for the definition of behaviour.

An object class describes a group of objects with similar properties, common behaviour and a common relationship to other objects. The objects listed above are likely to belong to the following (object) classes:

■ Order;
■ Company;
■ Employee;
■ TV Personality.

Defining these classes is one of the major tasks of object-oriented development. The usefulness of a class will vary from perspective (Larry the Lamb may be viewed as an employee by the television company) and are likely to change in nature as development progresses and more is learned about classes and how they interact with each other.

Object diagrams model objects, classes and their relationships to one another. A class diagram shows how object classes relate to each other and is analogous to the Logical Data Structures encountered earlier. Instance diagrams show how particular occurrences are related and are useful in discussing scenarios, clarifying rules and working through examples.

In Rumbaugh's *et al.* notation objects are shown in a 'soft box' and object classes in a rectangle (see figures 7.1 and 7.2). The class name is shown in parentheses at the top of the object box.

An attribute is a data value held by objects in that class. For example, number is an attribute of the object Order. Each attribute name is unique within a class but

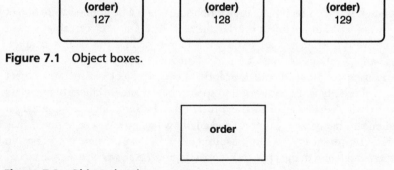

Figure 7.1 Object boxes.

Figure 7.2 Object class box.

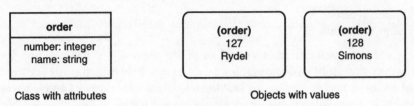

Class with attributes   Objects with values

Figure 7.3 Extended object and class notation.

not across all classes. Hence number may also be an attribute in the class Invoice. Attributes may be listed within the class box and can be supplemented by details of type and any default values that might apply. Class boxes have a line between the class name and the attributes. Object boxes do not have this line (see figure 7.3).

If the extended type notation is used it is helpful to declare a standard set. Cook and Daniels (1994) suggest the following value types:

- Number;
- Integer;
- String;
- Date;
- Time;
- Symbol.

Classes do not have to be given unique identifiers unless those identifiers exist in the real world. For example, order number is a legitimate identifier because it is used in the real world business function and usually appears on the physical order form. However, another object, such as Company, may not have any particular identifier – it may only contain descriptive attributes such as company name, address, contact, etc. In object terminology this is sufficient. We do not need to invent some identifier (such as company code) to uniquely identify a particular company. This concept is very useful because it means that we can handle more easily circumstances where identifiers are inappropriate, for example, standard paragraphs (in a text application), or garage layouts (in house design).

An operation is some function or transformation that can be applied to an object class. These are listed in the lower third of the class box. This area can also be used to show derived attributes – an issue we will return to later in this chapter. Attributes and operations are both termed features of the object.

A line is used to show the relationships between object classes and object instances. Multiplicity is the term used to specify how many instances of one class may relate to a single instance of another object class. In Rumbaugh's *et al.* notation a solid ball means many (zero or more) and a hollow ball means zero or one. Lines without balls represent exactly one. Multiplicity can also be shown by specific values if these are found in the application area. Figure 7.5 shows an example model and figure 7.6 summarizes the notation.

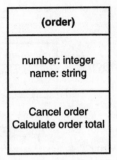

Figure 7.4   The object order.

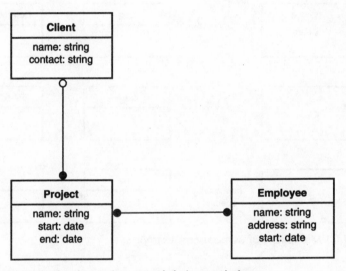

Figure 7.5   Example object classes and their associations.

In figure 7.6 the first example shows that a Delivery Note is on exactly one leg and that a leg (of a journey) has only one Delivery Note. This is slightly modified in the third example whereby further examination of the business has revealed that a Leg need not have a Delivery Note because the trailer can travel empty. In this particular application each leg can only have two locations (its source and destination) and so this can be explicitly noted in the model. Figure 7.7 gives the Object Model for this application with a Logical Data Structure for comparison.

It might also be recalled that the relationships on a Logical Data Structure could be named using a standard convention. Association lines can also be annotated using role labels although there does not appear to be any agreed convention for this.

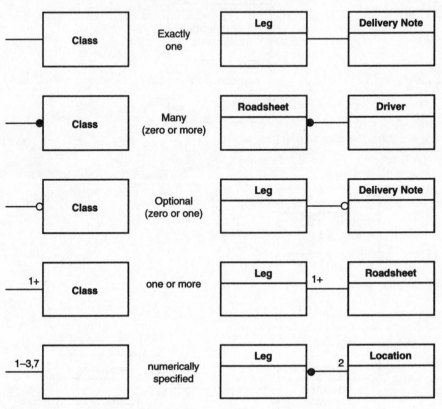

Figure 7.6 Multiplicity of associations: examples.

One-to-many relationships between entities in a Logical Data Structure are reflected by the presence of the foreign key in the entity at the many end of the relationship. For example, driver number (the identifier of Driver) would be held as a foreign key in Roadsheet to represent the relationship. It is generally accepted that this convention is not used in an object-oriented approach. Foreign keys are seen as a design decision to do with the implementation of the system using an RDBMS. However, this can cause a problem. The physical Roadsheet actually holds the driver number in the header section of the form and I think users would expect to see it on the Roadsheet object. They do not see it as a foreign key but as a data item they would expect to be held in that collection of attributes. On the other hand, this approach does make the notation more suitable for modelling a wider range of applications where the concept of identifiers and posting these identifiers is inappropriate. I can recall a text handling application I was involved in some years ago where standard paragraphs and sentences were given unique identifiers that were used in letters sent to individual customers. The Letter entity included the

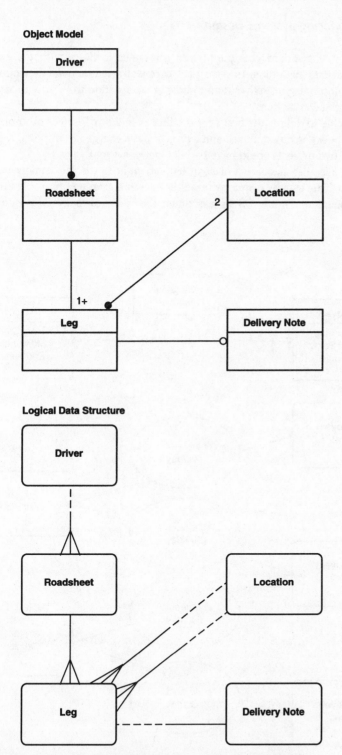

Figure 7.7   Object model and logical data structure compared.

foreign keys of standard paragraphs and sentences to fit in with the rules of conventional data modelling. In retrospect an object-oriented notation would have been much more useful, rather than forcing an application to fit in with standard data modelling conventions.

It is possible to define attributes for the link as in figure 7.8. For example, each association between an employee and a project has a chargeout property. A person working on two projects could have two distinct chargeout values.

The link may also become a class in its own right to resolve a many-to-many relationship. This usually occurs where there is more than one property attached to the association. Figure 7.9 breaks down the many-to-many encountered in figure 7.5.

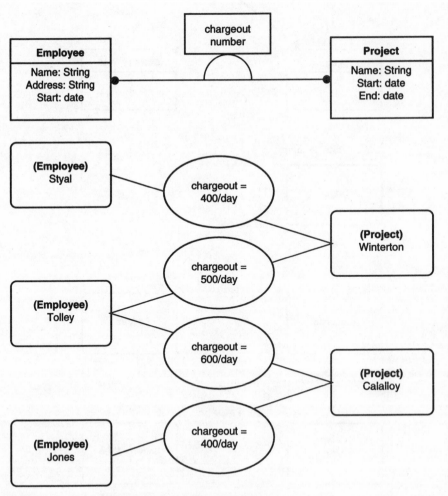

Figure 7.8 Association property with examples.

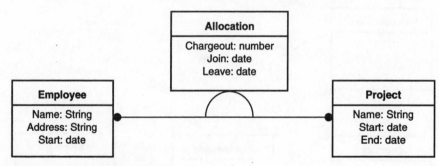

Figure 7.9 Association type.

7.4 Object principles

Two central principles of the object-oriented approach are abstraction and encapsulation. Abstraction is primarily concerned with appropriate classification. Booch (1994) defines it as 'the essential characteristics of an object that distinguishes it from all other kinds of objects and thus provide crisply defined conceptual boundaries, relative to the perspective of the user'.

Meyer's (1988) contractual model helps clarify this concept of abstraction. In his terminology he suggests that each object has a contractual agreement with all other objects it interacts with. This contract has defined pre-conditions and post-conditions. The conditions of the contract are broken if the pre-conditions are not provided by the supplier objects. In the example below (figure 7.10) a failure to provide vat-rate from VAT would provide the object Invoice Line with insufficient information to fulfil its contract. Similarly, the incorrect calculation of the line vat-amount (given the correct vat-rate and unit price) would mean that Invoice Line had broken its contract and that client objects of Invoice Line (such as Invoice) could not rely upon the results:

- **Encapsulation hides the detail of the implementation of an object**. 'No part of a complex system should depend upon the internal details of any other part' (Ingalls in Booch, 1994).
- **Abstraction and encapsulation are complementary concepts**. Encapsulation is often achieved through information hiding, keeping secret from all other objects the information they do not need to know. The implementation of the Invoice Line object may include:

    Line nett-price = prod-price × line-qty
    Line vat-amnt = Line nett-price × vat-rate

But the point is that the objects sending data to the Invoice Line (for example VAT object sending vat-rate) do not need to know how their information is used. This concept is close to that of cohesion and coupling described in the first edition of this book and considered again in chapter 8. Hence we are trying to identify strong

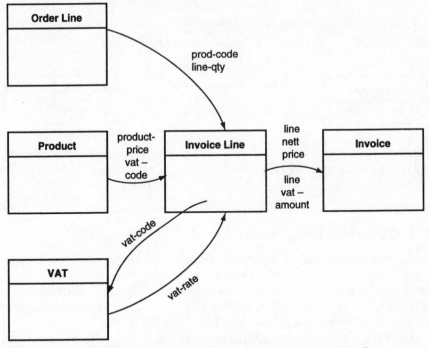

Figure 7.10 Contractual relationships between invoice and invoice line.

cohesive objects that are coupled only through exchanging data with other objects and do not need to know how these objects actually work.

Before moving onto further concepts of object-oriented development it is worth dwelling on the fundamental problem of abstraction. Classification is a problem in all things. We are basically looking for sameness, a common structure or behaviour that makes this set of things sufficiently different from another set. But even in scientifically rigorous disciplines classification is highly dependent upon the reasons for that classification. Furthermore, over time the basis of these classifications will be challenged and data reinterpreted to fit into new classifications.

Aggregation is usually referred to as a 'whole-part' or 'is-part-of' relationship where the whole is made up of the parts. Cook and Daniels (1994) further define aggregation to mean life-time dependency. The 'parts' are permanently attached to the 'whole' and cannot be removed from it without being destroyed. Conversely, destroying the 'whole' destroys the 'parts'. In figure 7.11 each Leg must be associated with a single Roadsheet. A Roadsheet has many (one or more) Legs. Aggregation is shown as a diamond placed on the association line next to the class that is the 'whole' or aggregate of the parts. In this case it is Roadsheet and this freezes this end of the association. If a Roadsheet is destroyed so are all the Legs.

Rumbaugh *et al.* (1991) believes that there are a number of associations where the use of aggregation is not clear cut. 'When in doubt', he writes 'use ordinary association.'

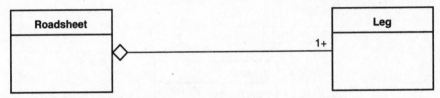

Figure 7.11   Aggregation relationship.

Inheritance defines a relationship between classes where one class shares the structure or behaviour defined in one (single inheritance) or more (multiple inheritance) other object classes. In this sense inheritance represents a hierarchy with a subclass inheriting from one or more superclasses. Semantically it may be defined as an 'is-a' relationship:

- Purchase Order is a kind of Order.
- Sales Order is a kind of Order.
- Debit Note is a kind of Invoice.

Thus we may define Order as an object that encapsulates data items and behaviour common to all orders. Standing Order, Sales Order and Purchase Order may all be defined with additional data items or behaviours.

In figure 7.12, Order is a superclass of Standing Order and Internal SO and External SO are subclasses of Standing Order. Each sub-class is said to inherit the features of its superclass. For example, Purchase Order inherits order number and order date from the superclass Order. The notation for inheritance is a triangle connecting a superclass to its subclasses. The superclass is connected by a line to the apex of the triangle. The subclasses are connected by lines to a horizontal bar along the base of the triangle.

Figure 7.12 (b) shows 7.12 (a) as conventional entities.

If all objects of Order conform to the sub-types Standing Order, Purchase Order and Sales Order then the supertype Order is said to be abstract and this can be specified within the object definition. If we can have an object that is an Order but is not a Standing Order, Purchase Order or Sales Order, then Order is not an abstract type – it has object instances of its own.

Sub-types can also be used to eliminate optional associations (see figure 7.13).

A subclass may override a superclass feature by defining a feature with the same name. This overriding feature may be used to tighten a specification or to specify behaviour associated only with that subclass.

Cook and Daniels (1994) define the abstract type of an object within the invariants sub-section of the object definition (see figure 7.14). An invariant is some Boolean condition (true or false) whose truth must always be upheld. They also use this area to hold information that we have tended to store in the logical Data Dictionary – such as value ranges and the rules for derived values. Interestingly, they have a neutral view about whether an attribute is stored or derived. They state that properties are not designs, just an indication that the object 'knows about' a value. The implementation of the property is of no interest at this stage, hence

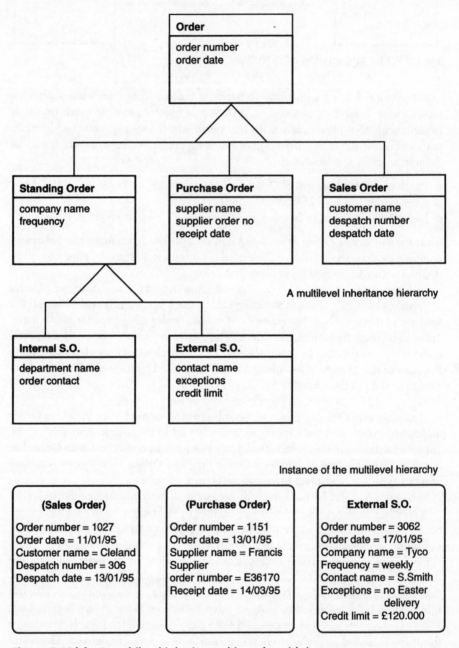

Figure 7.12(a) A multilevel inheritance hierarchy with instances.

SALES ORDER	**Sales-order-no** Customer-name Despatch-no Despatch-date Sales-order-date

PURCHASE ORDER	**Purchase-order-no** Purchase-order-date Supplier-name Supplier-order-no Receipt-date

INTERNAL STANDING ORDER	**Standing-order-no** Standing-order-date Company-name Frequency Department-name Order-contact

EXTERNAL STANDING ORDER	**Standing-order-no** Standing-order-date Company-name Frequency Contact-name Exceptions Credit-limit

Figure 7.12(b) Figure 7.12(a) represented as conventional entities.

'derived' has no meaning. We took a similar approach in the normalization of the project reporting system tables in chapter 5. This is again a very useful idea because it saves the time traditionally spent arguing about whether to hold a derived value. The answer is 'yes' and we can sort the detail out in later physical design.

In contrast, Rumbaugh *et al.* (1991) uses a slash in front of a derived attribute. For example:

/vat component
    {vat component = nett price × vat rate}

Both Rumbaugh *et al.* (1991) and Cook and Daniels (1994) also extend their notation to include constraints on and between associations. These extensions again place on the diagram, information that we would traditionally have kept in the Data Dictionary.

So far we have considered the structure of the objects and their expression in a representative notation. There are many similarities with conventional data

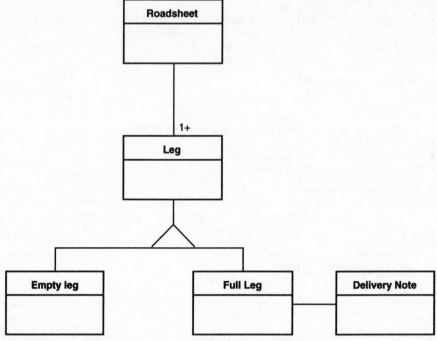

Figure 7.13   Eliminating optional relationships.

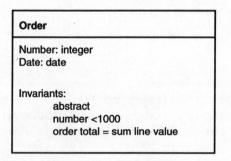

Figure 7.14   Invariants defined within the object class.

modelling but there are also differences caused by the concepts of aggregation, hierarchy, attribute naming and handling of 'derived' data. Associations are not implemented through foreign keys. Consequently the application of this approach is more natural for a wider range of applications (such as Computer Aided Design, text handling, etc.) than conventional data analysis with its orientation to RDBMS implementation.

7.5 Modelling object behaviour

We have also noted that behavioural elements are being included within the object definition rather than in a separate model. However, it is in the expression of object behaviour that object-oriented methodologies begin to diverge. Like structured methodologies most authors appear to generally agree on state definition and structure. It is in the expression of behaviour (process or events in the term used in these books up to now) that there appears to be less agreement.

In this introductory text we would like to consider three familiar possibilities.

- Entity Life Histories;
- Structured English;
- State Charts.

7.5.1 Entity Life Histories

These represent events within entities (objects) and so show how objects are created, modified and (if required) deleted. In addition, the ELH provides a graphical notation using familiar constructs. The State Indicators represent controls within the object to prevent or allow certain events to occur. We have found that modified ELHs (Object Life Histories) work well in conventional business data processing applications. In fact the absence of foreign keys in the object makes for a simpler life history. Similarly the less prescriptive perspective of 'derived' data means that there are less worries about how the calculation of this value will be implemented in the final design. Operations can be extended to include any verbs that may prove useful and the use of a separate Operations List leads to a relatively uncluttered diagram. Graham (1994) includes ELHs (and ECDs) in his SOMA method as possible models for showing how objects react to system events. Their under-use in the literature may be due to the preferred use of State Transition Diagrams by Real Time system developers.

7.5.2 Structured English or Action Diagrams

In chapter 6 Action Diagrams were introduced as a way of modelling the process or function across entities (or objects). Hence it appears the very anathema of object-oriented development. However, there is no reason why the constructs cannot be used within the object. For example, figure 7.15 is the Action Diagram for the Entity Life History shown in figure 6.8. In some respects the meaning of the State Indicators (such as for End of Year) are sometimes easier to express and understand in simple English condition statements.

Many object-oriented methodologies use Structured English type constructs within a formal notation. Meyer is a notable example. The action diagram of figure 7.15 highlights the fact that attributes of Customer (such as address and discount code) cannot be modified after entry. This can be addressed by adding a further Case statement in the DOWHILE changes section.

```
CASE   Customer detail changes
         Store customer-address, discount-code
```

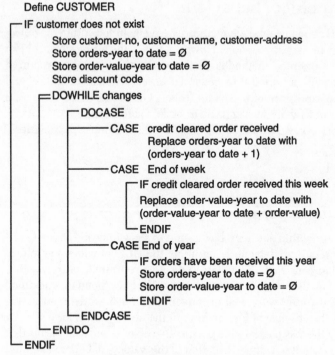

Define CUSTOMER
IF customer does not exist
    Store customer-no, customer-name, customer-address
    Store orders-year to date = Ø
    Store order-value-year to date = Ø
    Store discount code
    DOWHILE changes
        DOCASE
           CASE   credit cleared order received
               Replace orders-year to date with
               (orders-year to date + 1)
           CASE   End of week
               IF credit cleared order received this week
               Replace order-value-year to date with
               (order-value-year to date + order-value)
               ENDIF
           CASE End of year
               IF orders have been received this year
               Store orders-year to date = Ø
               Store order-value-year to date = Ø
               ENDIF
        ENDCASE
    ENDDO
ENDIF

Figure 7.15 Action diagram for the object customer.

7.5.3 State charts

The idea of a State Transition chart has been introduced in chapter 3. Like dialogues, objects can only be in certain states. Events occur that change the state of the object. These events can usually only occur in a certain sequence. For example, an Order might have the life-history defined in figure 7.16. In this representation each state is shown as a soft-box and each transition as an arrowed line with a short description of the event that causes the state change.

A Harel state chart is a powerful notation for describing states and the transitions that are allowed between states. The softbox is split into three sections (see figure 7.17). The arrow with the black blob on it tail shows the initial state of the object (in this case Placed). Figure 7.17 also shows further transitions for cancelling and amending orders. Notice that this is allowed up until the goods are sent. Once the order object is in the state Despatched it cannot be amended or cancelled.

The State chart allows nested states to reduce the number of transitions. Figure 7.18 introduces a new state Fulfilling to nest the Placed and Picked states. The transition cancel leaving the state applies to both the nested states. The amend transition also applies to both nested states and ends up at the state Placed. In fact the diagram now consists of three states Fulfilling, Cancelled and Despatched.

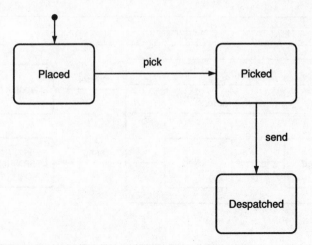

Figure 7.16 Initial state diagram for order object.

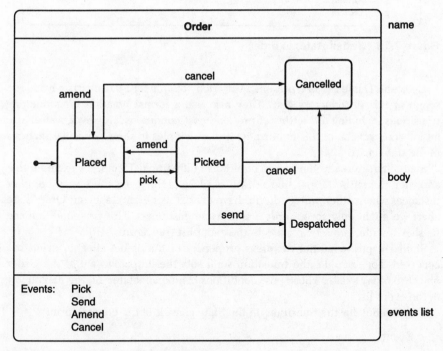

Figure 7.17 Initial state chart for order.

Consequently the diagram now requires two initial state arrows. One shows which state is its initial state (in this example Fulfilling), whereas the second shows which of the two nested states within this is the initial one (Placed).

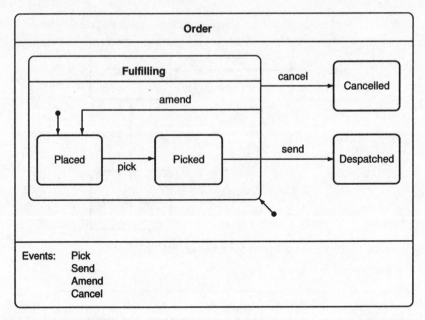

Figure 7.18   Nested states in order.

Cook and Daniels (1994) present a very rich notation for State charts beyond the scope of this introductory text. They also use a formal notation for modelling transitions including the setting of pre- and post-conditions. However, we can use an informal version of this in our next three examples to show particular features of the state chart.

State charts already show pre-conditions of a particular kind, for example that an order cannot be despatched until it is picked. However, there may be other instances where other pre-conditions have to exist. For example, in our Order state chart we might only accept orders from valid customers. This pre-condition can be shown within square brackets in the event list (see figure 7.19).

Similarly, post-conditions express properties of the object after an event has occurred. For example, the transition send sets the despatch date of the Order object to today's date. These post-conditions can be annotated on the diagram or in the event list.

The notation for the transition on the State chart is of the general form:

Event1 / Action1

The event name might be qualified by attributes or conditions. For example:

Send goods [if stock exists] / [Physical stock' = Physical Stock – order qty]

Post-conditions, can also be added to the initial state arrow of the state chart showing the initial values of the properties when the object is created. For example (figure 7.20), the object Customer may have order total = 0 and order value = 0

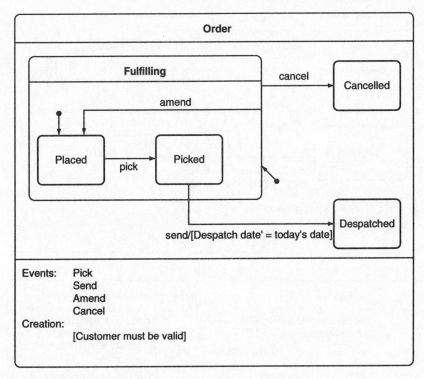

Figure 7.19 Pre- and post-conditions: order.

Part of a Statechart for Customer object showing post conditions of
the properties order value and order total for the initial state arrow

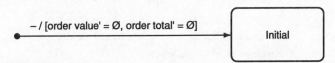

Figure 7.20 Post-condition.

at this point. Cook and Daniels append a prime character (') to show that it is the
new value of the property.

Post-conditions are also enclosed within squares brackets.

Some events cause the destruction of objects. This is shown in figure 7.21. Orders
can be deleted if they are cancelled or more than 7 years old.

State charts (and State Transition charts in general) are very applicable in the
Real Time system environment. In fact Ward and Mellor (1985) specifically
introduced them in this context in their extension to Tom deMarco's original data
flow diagramming notation. However, Graham (1994), reviewing the Fusion Method

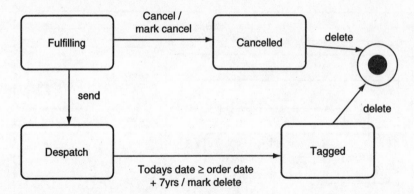

Figure 7.21 The destruction of the object order.

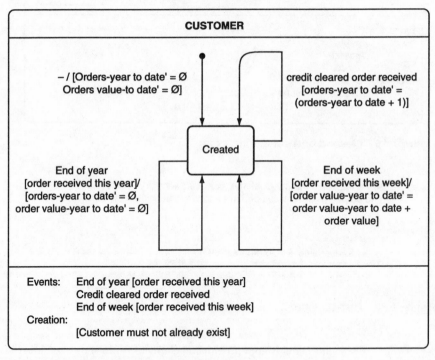

Figure 7.22 State chart for customer.

(Coleman *et al.*, 1994) reports that the dynamic model of Rumbaugh's OMT method was not found to be useful in practice. Graham (1994) notes that this is:

> an encouraging if remarkable finding compared to conventional wisdom, which makes me suspect that excessive emphasis on state models is the result of telecomms and real-time application backgrounds.

Indeed the problem of applying a State chart to an information system is partly shown by figure 7.22. There is really only one state of Customer and so the chart is relatively uninteresting However, it does provide an alternative perspective and you might like to compare the representation with the Entity Life History (figure 6.8) and the Action Diagram (figure 7.15).

7.6 Summary

This chapter has looked at object-oriented development from the perspective of state and behaviour. As Ian Graham has noted: In dealing with things object-oriented we must also realize that we are entering an area that is not well bounded and where research is still incomplete in certain areas. Graham has identified probably well over 60 more or less complete object-oriented methods in existence in his comprehensive review of the subject.

It is likely that different methods will merge and also become integrated into established methods such as SSADM and Information Engineering. The most interesting area will again be behaviour definition. State charts are particularly useful because they allow the early expression of business control rules (such as 'orders cannot be amended after they have been picked'), which have not been particularly well dealt with by other models.

A particular strength of the object-oriented approach is its application in environments that cannot be successfully represented by models oriented to a database solution.

8 Physical Design

8.1 Introduction

The objective of physical design is to define the physical data structure and the physical programs that will use this data structure to fulfil the requirements of the system. This physical specification should utilize the chosen implementation environment efficiently and effectively and adhere to installation standards. The variation in potential implementation environments necessarily means that the approach to physical design cannot be tightly prescribed. Different criteria may apply for different styles of implementation (3GL or 4GL for instance) and also for different implementation systems (CODASYL or Relational Database Management Systems).

This chapter gives a general view of the issues that arise in moving from logical to physical design and considers the usefulness of some of the logical models to particular implementation environments. It begins by concentrating on data design issues.

8.2 Logical and physical data design

Physical data design should attempt to minimize the following factors:

- Data access times;
- Processing times;
- Use of backing store;
- System development time;
- System maintenance time;
- The need for database reorganization;
- System and user interface complexity.

These factors frequently conflict. For example, the use of backing store may be reduced at the cost of system complexity and perhaps increased maintenance times. Trends in hardware and software costs suggest that the physical design should be based upon the following assumptions:

- Backing store costs are less significant than development and maintenance costs.
- Run times and response times should be minimized to satisfy user interface and operational requirements.
- Development and maintenance costs should be minimized.
- The end-user interface should be kept as simple as possible particularly when physical data is being manipulated directly by the user using advanced DBMS features.

The last of these objectives may be best achieved by maintaining a one-to-one mapping between the logical and physical designs. If end-user query facilities (Query-by-Example: QBE or Query-by-Forms: QBF) are to be used then the database structures may be visible to the user and hence should be kept as simple as possible. This places a significant limitation upon the degree of optimization possible. If the DBMS permits the user to see a logical view of the system that is different from the actual implementation without critical performance penalties the problem is more tractable. For instance many RDBMS's permit the definition of views that may be derived from several physical tables.

The Required System LDM supported by normalized relations represents an unambiguous and implementation-free description of the data. This is a more accessible and stable view for the user than the description of the actual physical file structures. This separation of logical and physical perspectives should make maintenance easier. Changes that are only concerned with physical database access may be performed without any change to the logical processing and vice versa.

If the application system meets the user's performance requirements unnecessary optimization may also have unsatisfactory long-term side-effects. Optimization, by its very nature, may destroy the one-to-one correspondence between the logical model and the physical implementation. Unlike the logical model the physical design may have to be biased to optimize the performance of one set of transactions at the expense of another set. This almost inevitably makes the application system less flexible and maintainable.

The logical model of the system has been developed so that it is:

- Clear and unambiguous;
- Free from unnecessary redundancy;
- Easy to enhance and extend.

Consequently, we would like to carry over these advantages into our physical design and make each entity into its physical equivalent – a file, table, set, etc. However, it may be impossible to implement the logical model without modification because of performance constraints or limitations of the target hardware or software.

8.3 Optimizing using facilities of the hardware and software

Wherever possible optimization should utilize the features of the file management software to satisfy agreed performance criteria. The one-to-one correspondence between physical and logical models should only be disturbed as a last resort.

Storage requirements may be minimized by using such features as:

- Variable length data items;
- Space compression in textual fields;
- Variable length records;
- Adjustment of block size and access methods.

Performance criteria may also be achieved by optimizing access to data storage by:

- **Placing details near their master entity occurrences**. It may be very useful to place Order Line records near their header details held in Order. Many Relational DBMS products support a 'place near' facility sometimes through a cluster index. CODASYL DBMS implementations have a *VIA SET* command that places member records as close as possible to their owners. For example, if an owner (Order) has six members (Order Lines) then all occurrences may be placed on the same page (block) of the disk and so all seven occurrences are retrieved within a single disk access. An alternative implementation through the CALC command would lead to all seven occurrences being distributed throughout the database and the same operation could require seven disk accesses.
- **Appropriate selection of file (table) organization and access method**. A number of options are available for storing the physical order of occurrences (records) within the table. These include:
- *Serial* order. New rows (records) are added to the bottom of the tables regardless of what these rows contain. Record order is essentially transaction order.
- *Sequential* tables. These contain records stored in order of the primary key. Records added to the file are stored at the physical end of the file until it is re-sorted into key sequence.

In serial and sequential files individual records can only be found by reading the whole file until the required key value is located.

File organizations that allow more direct access to individual records include:

- *Indexed sequential*. In this method records are also maintained in key sequence but have an index structure built on top of the actual data. The structure of an indexed sequential file is shown in figure 8.1. The master index is the highest level index that contains pointers down to the next lower level index, the cylinder indexes. Several indexes may be constructed for each set of data records. If the index is ordered in the same key sequence as the data it is called the primary index. All other indexes are ordered in a different sequence from the data records and are called alternate or secondary indexes.

  Locating a particular record is achieved by following the index tree from the master index or root to the target data block. The block containing the target record is then read in order to locate the record with a matching key. If this search is unsuccessful then the record will be found in the associated overflow area. This

1000 records are stored sequentially in blocks of 8.
Each index block contains 100 entries.

Master Index

Record key	Block address
Dixon	950
Mason	951
Wroe	952

Cylinder Index

Record key / Block address					
950	Aylesbury	1000	Barrett	1001	Dixon	1002
951	King	1021	Lindon	1022	Mason	1024
952	Tyson	1036	Wroe	1041		

Data records (keys shown for illustration purposes only)

1000	Abbey	Anderson	Anderton	Ashton	Aylesbury			
1001	Baard	Babbage	Bait	Bamford	Barnacle	Barnes	Barnett	Barrett
1002	Chiswick	Cristal	Dixon					
1003								
1027	Badley							

Figure 8.1 Indexed sequential organization.

requires the reading of at least one further block of data (as in the case of Badley in figure 8.1). Some blocks in this structure are not full, because an allowance for expansion was made when the file was created. Insertion of a new record must be undertaken in the correct location in the correct sequence. If the appropriate block is full then one or more records with higher key values must be pushed out of the primary data block and into the overflow area.

Indexed sequential files are generally slower than direct files (see below) since the time taken to traverse the index tree is greater than that needed to hash a record key to find its address. Storing various indexes also consumes disk space. However it is a very flexible method of file organization because it offers the facility for both sequential (record order) and random (by indexes) access.

- A *relative* file. This is a self-addressing file in which any individual record can be accessed directly. The file may be thought of as a serial string of areas, each capable of holding a logical record. Each one of these areas is denominated by a relative record number. Record storage and retrieval is based on this number. For example, the tenth record is the one addressed by the relative record number ten, and will be held in the tenth record area whether or not records have been written in any of the previous areas. Whatever the size of the file only one disk read or write operation is required to find any record.

  In this type of organization records can be quickly accessed anywhere in the file by simply using the record key as the address and records can also be inserted, updated and deleted anywhere and not just at the end. Relative files never need reorganizing as the organization takes place when they are initially created. It is also possible to access sequentially a relative file by reading the records in the order they are stored.

  However, the main disadvantage is that each potential record has a space reserved for it and hence the disk may be relatively empty, particularly at times when there are few physical records active.

- A *direct* file. This is one where the key is transformed in some way to the physical address of the record on the device. Unlike a relative file it does not require the key to be an integer (so character and alphanumeric fields can be used) and the address is a bucket not a record space.

  Direct files also provide better space utilization where there are gaps in the chosen record key. The amount of space available to the file is determined by the efficiency of the hashing algorithm. Hashing is a technique in which the record key is converted into another value that serves as a storage address. The block found at this address should include the target record, if it exists. All records within a block are physically adjacent to each other as in a serial file. If the target record is not in the block then it may be located in a specified overflow area. Figure 8.2 shows how a simple hashing algorithm is applied to a selection of records to find their storage location on the disk. In this example the position of the required record is found by dividing the record key by 19 and using the remainder to point to the location address. Each block contains five records.

  The overall performance of a direct file is determined by the number of likely collisions that occur (as in the record with key 4771, which must be stored in the overflow area). In such circumstances the hashing algorithm produces the same address for two records and hence one of these has to be given a new address in an overflow area. This leads to additional disk accesses that results in slower performance.

  The main disadvantage of this method is the inability to read records sequentially. It is possible to start at the first block and access all its records, read the next block and retrieve its records, and so on. However the records will not be physically stored within a block in key sequence and so processes demanding the retrieval of records within a range of dates or account numbers will be extremely slow to execute.

Record Block
key address Block Key Data

Record key	Block address		Block	Key	Data				
1001	13		0	6612	data				
1291	18		1						
6612	0		2	2206	data	2472	data	1731	data
2206	2		3	1941	data				
2472	2		4						
1941	3		5						
1731	2		6	1279	data				
7712	17		7						
1591	14		8						
4771	2		9	6241	data				
5431	16		10						
1279	6		11						
6241	9		12						
			13	1001	data				
Hashing algorithm:			14	1591	data				
Division by 19 –			15						
block address is			16	5431	data				
the remainder			17	7712	data				
			18	1291	data				
			19	4771	data				
overflow {			20						
			21						

Figure 8.2 A direct file: hashed on the record key.

- *Inverted* files. These are organized so that records may be retrieved by giving values of any data item in the record structure. An index is kept for each data item value, or data item range, and holds an entry for each record processing that value or range.

   The structure enables quick response to queries on non-key fields. Figure 8.3 shows an inverted file structure for a Book file. It has been partially inverted on the attributes selling-price, author and publisher-name. It is therefore easy to answer such questions as:

- Which books are in the range £10–20 selling price?
- Which books are stocked for the author L. Payne?
- Which stocked books are by the publisher 'NCC'?

Further opportunities for enhancing performance may be gained through:

- Implementation of key only entities as indexes;
- Providing secondary indexes for foreign keys;
- Providing indexes for non-key data items used frequently for access;

Selling price directory	
Key	Pointer
0–5	
6–10	1,2,3
11–20	4,5
21–30	6
>30	

Author directory	
Key	Pointer
A Parkin	1,
S Jones	2,
L Payne	4,5,12

Publisher directory	
Key	Pointer
NCC	1,2,4
Arnold	3,5
Wiley	6,45

Block	Book key	File data	
		title	cost-price
1	21	Systems Analysis	9.50
2	22	Systems Design	9.40
3	24	Data Analysis	7.50
4	25	Data Security	12.00
5	26	Security	12.50
6	29	Artificial Intelligence	25.00
7			
8			
9			
10			
11			
12	45	Networks	12.50

Figure 8.3   A partially inverted file.

- Building required indexes at the run-time of a process;
- Providing a direct access mechanism to detail occurrences;
- Holding small reference tables in main memory during process execution.

It is also important to check that when the physical design is optimized with respect to one process the speed of execution for other processes has not been inadvertently reduced to an unacceptable level.

8.4 Optimizing by tuning the logical model

If the implementation facilities of the software do not offer sufficient improvement in performance it will be necessary to compromise the structure of the physical model so that its design is no longer exactly the same as the Logical Data Model. Tuning the physical model to satisfy specific performance targets in this way may produce a system which is more difficult to maintain and less easily supports *ad hoc* user queries and functional changes.

Tuning may include combining logically separate entities to reduce the number of database accesses for a particular transaction. For example, the partial Logical Data Model shown in figure 8.4 shows two entities Customer Type and Customer. These have the following attributes:

CUSTOMER TYPE
Customer-type-code
Customer-type-description

CUSTOMER
Customer-no
Customer-name
*Customer-type-code

It transpires that the processes using these entities always require access to the Customer Type entity to print the type description in full. One of these processes does not currently meet its performance target and so the decision is taken to merge these two entities into one Customer file with the following data items:

CUSTOMER file
Customer-no
Customer-name
Customer-type-code
Customer-type-description

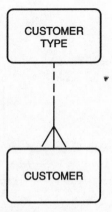

Figure 8.4 Partial logical data model.

This has de-normalized the data (in fact it is now in Second Normal Form but not Third) in a controlled way. The designer is aware of the unnecessary redundancy this will create and the problem of updating descriptions but is willing to pay this price for the benefit of performance. The map between the entities and the files is maintained and is shown in figure 8.5. All future discussions with the users about these entities will focus on the Logical Data Model not the physical file design. However, the map will quickly show the designers the physical ramifications of any change in the logical design.

Performance may also be improved by introducing redundant or derived data in the form of counts or totals or duplicating data in more than one table to reduce the access path or the number of accesses for a particular transaction.

The problem discussed above could also have been solved by simply duplicating the customer-type-description in the Customer file and leaving a type file with the following fields:

> CUSTOMER TYPE file
> **Customer-type-code**
> Customer-type-description

In this instance the main purpose of the Customer Type file is data entry. A program will need to be written to cascade all changes made in this file down into the Customer file. This solution would be particularly useful if one of the requirements is to print off a list of type codes and their meaning.

The issue of derivable data was also discussed in chapter 5. It is at this stage that we would review the advantages and disadvantages of holding fields such as line-value, order-value, etc. Cumulative fields might also be considered. The need to

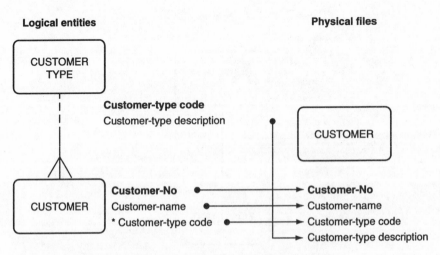

Figure 8.5 Mapping between logical entities and physical files.

provide telephone order clerks with customer orders-year-to-date and value-orders-year-to-date can be satisfied by reading all orders for that customer and calculating the relevant totals. However, this might be desperately slow and produce a response time completely inappropriate for a clerk taking the order over the telephone. Consequently we may introduce cumulative fields into the file design so that these queries can be answered very quickly. This introduces redundant data and adds some complications to the process design. It should also be re-called that cancellations may lead to reductions in the cumulative figure and also there will now be the need to provide end-of-year clear down routines. However, performance might demand that we make these physical compromises.

CUSTOMER file
Customer-no
Customer-name
*Customer-type-code
Customer-type-description
Orders-year-to-date
Order-value-year-to-date

Performance can also be improved by splitting entities into two or more physical files.

This split can be vertical (shown in figure 8.6) or horizontal (as in figure 8.7). The

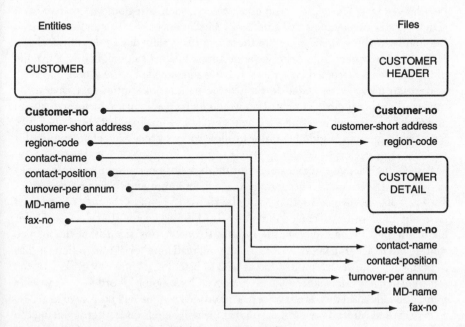

Figure 8.6 Vertical splitting of the customer entity.

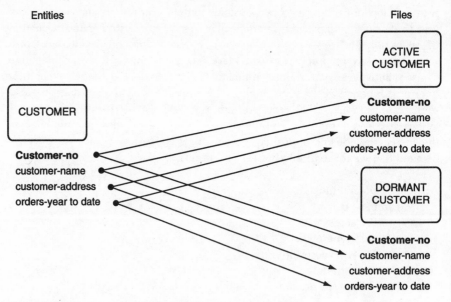

Figure 8.7 Horizontal splitting of the customer entity.

vertical split essentially places little used descriptive fields in a separate file. This creates a smaller active file for the main transactions to access. The same result can be achieved by splitting the file on other criteria, such as region, salesman or even activity. Statistics may show that a relatively small number of customers are accessed frequently by the system. Access to these records is slow due to the physical size of the file. Consequently, it might be appropriate to create a small highly active file of the frequently accessed customers, leaving a larger file for the others.

Relationships can be added to reduce the number of entities that have to be traversed during the transaction. This would involve adding a new foreign key to an entity and perhaps creating a triangle of relationships like that shown in figure 8.8. Here region-no is added to order to allow speedy processing of an enquiry for regional sales performance.

Postponing database updates and storing them in transaction files for later off-line processing is a relatively common strategy for improving system performance. For example, an invoice routine has to be run at the end of the week to request payment for all orders received in that week. Orders could be stored on the Order file when they are entered into the system. However, this means that the invoice routine has to access a large file for a relatively small number of transactions. It has to perform a date search on that file as well as batching together all orders for the same customer. Performance may be improved by keeping all orders on a weekly transaction file until they are invoiced. The invoice routine will only have to access a very small file and all transactions on that file will be relevant. After invoicing the orders are moved to the main Order file and the weekly transaction file archived

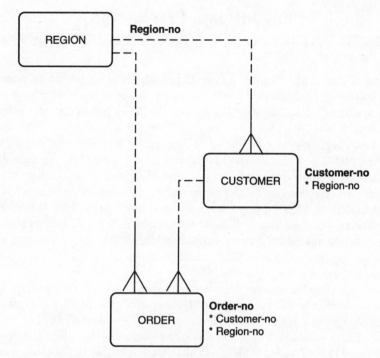

Figure 8.8 Triangular relationship for faster access.

or deleted. However, in such a solution the designer must ensure that reports and queries requiring order totals must read both the main order and weekly transaction file.

Performance can also be enhanced by establishing flag and indicator fields to eliminate unnecessary accesses. This can be demonstrated by returning to the invoicing example given above. The process must produce an invoice for all customers who have placed an order in that week. If the idea of a transaction file is rejected then an alternative might be to set a flag on all Customer records for which there has been an order in that week. These flags would be set to N at the start of the week and changed to Y on receipt of an order. The invoicing routine would only access customers with a Y flag and it would know that an invoice must be created for that customer because there will at least one relevant order on the Order file. On successful completion of the invoice routine the flags are re-set to N.

Once the database structure has been optimized it is important to examine all processes again to ensure that optimizing for one process has not had a disastrous effect on the performance of other processes. Optimization is concerned with making the most appropriate series of compromises for the requirements of the application. These compromises are recorded on a map that shows the relationship of the business model (Logical Data Model) and the physical file design.

8.5 Implications for data base design

A data base is a shared, formally defined, centrally controlled collection of data used in an organization.

Sharing of data is the ability of different applications to access the same piece of data, concurrently if necessary, without being aware of each other's existence. Sharing also means that new applications can be developed to operate against the same stored data.

In an application-centred approach to data processing there is little opportunity to share data. Each application has its own private files with the content and organization developed to suit that application. If applications try to share the same data there will be conflicting access requirements, different applications will require access to data in differing sequences and by different keys. This desired access flexibility is beyond the limited facilities provided by most file management systems of conventional operating systems. Similarly, difficulties occur in trying to exploit the data held in the application files, particularly when *ad hoc* reports need to access data across two or more application files.

Existing application files may lack data items required for new applications or may not be accessible in the way required. Consequently, the development of a new application requires that new application files be developed specifically for that application. This may require two or more files, or copies of the files, being reorganized and merged to form the new file. Difficulties may arise due to the inconsistencies in the duplicated data, which may not be easy to resolve. Duplication of data is bound to occur with application-centred files as data is rarely unique to one application.

Inconsistencies between duplicated data may be due to one file being updated but not another, this may be a factor of time in that one file is updated at more frequent time intervals than another, or may be due to errors in the operating procedures.

If integrating application files can remove duplication then the duplication is redundant. Only if there is a centralized awareness of the data requirements for each application can the redundancy of stored data be controlled. As long as duplicate copies of data exist there is the possibility of those copies becoming inconsistent.

Besides the duplication of data in application files there will also be duplication of data definition, integrity constraints and process definitions in many of the application programs. Should any of the application files or application processes be changed in any way the maintenance effort in editing, recompiling and retesting the application programs affected can be considerable.

With a database approach the definition of data is separated from the application program and formally defined by a central authority in a way that is suitable for all applications. If changes have to be made they are made once to the single definition, which is available to all application programs.

The concept of central control implies that there is some identifiable person, or group of persons, charged with the responsibility of deciding the information content of the data base, the storage structure and the access strategy, liaising with users, defining security and integrity checks, strategy for backup and recovery, and monitoring performance and changing requirements. This person or group of persons is normally termed the Data Base Administration (DBA).

The main advantages of a data base approach to data processing, as opposed to an application-centred approach, include the better exploitation of the data resource, enforcement of standards, controlled redundancy, improved integrity and security of data and reduced program maintenance. The disadvantages are the size, complexity and cost of a data base management system, the possible requirement of additional hardware, the higher impact of a failure and the greater complexity in recovery following a failure.

8.5.1 Data base management system

In order that the objectives of a data base system be fulfilled a generalized software package is required, this package is termed the Data Base Management System (DBMS). The role of the DBMS is to organize the data in the data base according to the given data definition and to provide access to the data for the different application programs and queries in a way that complies with the different user views of the data.

Each DBMS will have a specified way in which the data is structured, a language or languages to describe the structure of the data, a language or languages to access and manipulate the data in the data base and a set of procedures or utilities to maintain, monitor and tune the data base.

A DBMS must address the issue of data independence. The ANSI/SPARC Study Group on DBMS proposed an architecture for this purpose. The architecture is divided into three general levels representing three different views of the data.

- **The conceptual view.** This is a representation of the entire information content of the data base. Such a view consists of a description of record types, each of which is derived from a real world entity, and the relationships between the record types. This is a fairly stable, long-term view of the data that is capable of evolving with the organization.
- **The external view.** This is the way that the data is viewed by the application programs and users. There may be many external views each defining that part of the conceptual data that a given application requires. An external view is derived from the conceptual view but may redefine the format of data items, form aggregates and define sequencing but cannot override the constraints of the conceptual view. It is through the external view that the DBMS is able to maintain logical data independence.
- **The internal view.** This is a description of how the data is to be stored. It describes the device-oriented and access-oriented aspects such as device usage, block sizes, record formats, indexes and file structures. It is through the definition of the internal view that the DBMS is able to maintain physical data independence, which in particular will allow performance tuning.

It is the job of the DBMS to map between the various views of the data when access is made to the data base. In practice not all DBMS provide these logically separate views of the data.

There are two ways in which the data in the data base may be accessed. The first is by an application program written in a suitable high-level language (e.g. COBOL) and the second is direct access of the data base using a query facility. Both require a special language that may or may not be the same. In the first case the commands of the language will be embedded within the application program and may be compiled into the object program or simply interpreted at run time.

There are three accepted models on which the vast majority of DBMS are based, the hierarchical model, the network model and the relational model. These models, described below, are alternative ways of organizing or viewing data at the conceptual or logical level irrespective of machine implementation and storage.

8.5.1.1 Hierarchical data base model. The hierarchical model supports an inverted tree structure.

A tree consists of nodes connected by branches. The root node is at the top and its descendants below it. A parent node appears immediately above its children. There is only one root node and each child node can only have a single parent. Each node is always accessed through its parent.

IBM's Information Management System (IMS) is one DBMS that is based on the hierarchical model. First released by IBM in 1968 IMS has, over the years, been enhanced by additional features, improved performance and has accommodated advances in hardware. Data Language/I (DL/I) is the data base access and manipulation component of IMS.

At first sight the hierarchical structure (with its restriction of only one parent per child) suggests that it is highly unlikely that the Logical Data Model can be represented without modification. However, it is possible to build logical relationships between the child node of one tree structure and one other parent of a different tree structure. This is achieved through pointers that are still subject to a number of restrictions:

- Every segment, except root segments, must have one physical parent segment.
- A given segment can have at most one logical parent segment.
- A root segment cannot be a logical child.
- A logical child segment cannot be also be a logical parent segment.

This means that it is likely that the designer using a hierarchical database management system will have to make compromises in the design due to restrictions of the software rather than just because of performance alone.

For applications with a natural hierarchical data structure the hierarchical data model is a simple solution. Moreover, only a small number of commands are needed to navigate the data base and performance is good for applications that have fixed predefined hierarchical relationships.

However, modifying the physical structure of the data base is difficult and physical data independence is minimal; physical restructuring can cause modification to the program logic.

8.5.1.2 Network data base model. A system technically falls within the general network model if its underlying data structure is a simple network. A simple network is just a collection of records connected by one-to-many relationships.

In late 1971 the CODASYL Data base Task Group (DBTG) published a report detailing a specification for languages that define and process data. Although this report was not accepted as an official standard a number of vendors developed systems that followed these guidelines. Such systems have come to be called CODASYL systems based on the CODASYL model of a simple network. The initial proposal has undergone subsequent developments and refinements, some of them significant. However, the fundamental architecture and functional capability has remained much the same. A number of CODASYL systems are commercially available, including IDS/II from Honeywell Information Systems and IDMS from Cullinet software.

Although recent CODASYL reports essentially support the three levels or views of data, the earlier reports and most commercial systems do not. The conceptual data definition and many of the physical details are included in the *schema* and a *subschema* represents the external view of the data. There is a third definition that describes the remaining physical details.

Three languages are defined for data definition: the schema Data Definition Language, (schema DDL), the subschema Data Definition Language, (subschema DDL), and the Device Media Control Language, (DMCL), subsequently renamed the Data Storage Description Language (DSDL).

Programs accessing the data base can be written in one of the high-level languages, for example COBOL, with additional commands specific to the processing of the data base embedded in the code. These commands constitute the Data Manipulation Language (DML).

The CODASYL model does provide a degree of logical data independence, in that an application program whose subschema does not reference a new record type or a changed record type does not have be changed. However, a reasonable degree of physical data independence is achieved, although some changes to the physical structure can cause reduced performance, which can only be off-set by making changes to the program code.

The structure of a CODASYL database can be complex, especially to the casual user. but there are no real limitations on the types of data relationships that can be represented. In contrast to the hierarchical model the Logical Data Model can be implemented directly and will only have to be modified because of performance requirements. The only slight change is that foreign keys do not have to be included because the schema defines these through owners and members. So, for example, customer-no does not have to be stored within Order, relationship is established by the SET statement. A stylized CODASYL type schema is listed below:

```
AREA NAME IS SALES_PROCESSING

RECORD NAME IS CUSTOMER
  LOCATION MODE IS CALC
    USING CUSTOMER_NO
    DUPLICATES ARE NOT ALLOWED
  WITHIN SALES_PROCESSING

    CUSTOMER_NO
    CUSTOMER_NAME
    CUSTOMER_ADDRESS

RECORD NAME IS ORDER
  LOCATION MODE IS CALC
    USING ORDER_NO
    DUPLICATES ARE NOT ALLOWED
  WITHIN SALES_PROCESSING

    ORDER_NO
    ORDER_DATE

SET NAME IS CUSTOMER_ORDER
  OWNER IS CUSTOMER
    SET IS PRIOR PROCESSABLE
    ORDER IS PERMANENT INSERTION IS LAST
  MEMBER IS ORDER
    INSERTION IS AUTOMATIC
    LINKED TO OWNER
    SET SELECTION FOR CUSTOMER_ORDER
      IS THRU CUSTOMER_ORDER
      OWNER IDENTIFIED BY APPLICATION
```

Application programs written to interact with a CODASYL DBMS are complex in that they have to provide for the navigation through the records and sets of the subschema used by the program. Many CODASYL systems include query languages but in most cases the user is still expected to direct the navigation of the data base.

A large number of application systems have been developed using CODASYL systems and because of the speed that can be achieved they are likely to remain in use for some time to come.

8.5.1.3 Relational DBMS. The relational data base model first proposed by E. F. Codd in a paper in 1970 is significantly different in approach to the other data base models. It views the data as a simple collection of two-dimensional tables (or flat files) called *relations*. All the values in a column are values of the same *attribute type* and must also contain only a single attribute value. Each column of the table must have a distinct name, called the attribute name, and consequently the order of the columns in the table is immaterial. Each row of the table must be distinct, so that a row can always be identified by quoting an appropriate combination of attribute values, and consequently the order of the rows is also immaterial. The combination of attributes should be non-redundant that is no attribute can be omitted from the combination without destroying its ability to uniquely identify each row of data in the table. Such a combination of attributes is termed a *primary key*. There may be more than one such combination of attributes, each is termed a *candidate key*.

Codd originally specified two data manipulation languages called data sub-languages, one of which (relational calculus) was based on predicate calculus. The importance of this language is that it is used to measure the relational complete-ness of other relational languages, that is, it is a yardstick against which to measure the effectiveness of those languages.

Other relational DML languages, for example Query-by-Example, have been proposed and some of them implemented. The most important of these is called Structured Query Language (SQL), which has now been adopted as the standard language for relational data bases.

SQL is not just a data manipulation language, it also conforms to one of the other rules, later defined by Codd, that there should be at least one language that supports both data definition and data manipulation. Data manipulation is performed such that the answer to queries is also a table, that is, processing is performed a table-at-a-time, rather that a record-at-a-time, as in the hierarchical and network models. One advantage of this is that the system can optimize the execution of a query depending on what current storage structures are defined. Thus allowing a higher degree of physical data independence than in the other two models.

SQL can be used to define and create the *base relations* of the data base, which is equivalent to the conceptual level in the ANSI/SPARC model. SQL can also be used to define *views*, which are virtual tables derived from one or more of the base relations. Although views may form part of an external view of the data base, a user is more likely to require access to a combination of base tables and views.

Views provide logical data independence. If the data base structure is changed, columns added, relationships changed, in such a way that the view can still be derived from existing data, the user can still access the same view. A view should contain only the columns and rows that a user needs to see, consequently the view acts as a security mechanism. Views enable the same data to be viewed by users in different ways and since a view contains only the data required by the user his or her view of the data base is greatly simplified.

SQL can also be used to define additional physical storage structures in the form of indexes. Indexes can be defined (or dropped) on any column or combination of columns. Also the logical structure of the table can be altered by the addition of columns or by changing the format of existing columns. Such modification should not affect the logic of existing applications and so physical data independence is achieved.

There are now a number of relational data base implementations available, for example, INGRES from CA, ORACLE from Oracle Corp. and DB2 from IBM, all using SQL as the data manipulation language. Not all have implemented all aspects of the relational model as defined by Codd, in particular there are omissions in the area of integrity constraints. Some have defined additional features to the basic model, for example INGRES allows the user to define alternative storage structures for tables using SQL while still maintaining physical data independence.

The simplicity of the relational model makes it easy to understand and to use. The user does not need to be concerned with the physical structure of the data base so user requests can be non-procedural. The system optimizes the execution of each query. The model provides a high level of data independence, so both the physical structure and the logical structure can be changed without affecting the application programmers or users. However, poor performance has been the biggest disadvantage of this model but as it is the focus of a great deal of research, significant advances in data base technology are most likely to occur with this model.

Simple rules can be given for implementing the Logical Data Model with an RDBMS.

- Each entity in the LDS becomes a table. Each table is in third normal form.
- Each table is indexed by its primary key.
- Each compound-key table is indexed by each element of its compound key.
- Indexes are defined for each foreign key and each non-key access requirement.

Thus there is a very direct relationship between our logical model and an RDBMS implementation. In the RDBMS relationships between tables are represented by foreign keys, just as in the Relational Data Analysis of chapter 5.

8.6 Data and process design

Development methods increasingly reflect the interrelationship between process and data design. The processes have to manipulate the data as efficiently as demanded by the application requirements. This inevitably means that data design must proceed with one eye on process design and vice versa. This overlap is further blurred by current implementation strategies made possible by sophisticated software like modern Relational Database Management Systems (RDBMS). Such systems can, to some extent, not only manage the data but also the associated processing. Processes may only operate upon the data within certain business rules or integrity constraints, which are determined by the application and are identified during requirements.

These integrity constraints may be implemented in two ways. The first is to implement them directly in the procedures possibly using common routines for constraints that need to be enforced in several different circumstances. Thus the implementation of the integrity constraints is distributed among the procedures.

This may have some undesirable consequences:

- It is difficult to verify that all the requirements have been implemented.

■ Modification to these business rules is a greater and more hazardous maintenance task.

Alternatively the integrity constraints may be defined using the facilities of a RDBMS. Many RDBMS's have Data Dictionaries that provide automatic data validation at the type level. For instance, the RDBMS only permits the entry of numeric values if the entry field has been defined as numeric or valid dates if the field has been defined as a date field. RDBMS dictionaries increasingly provide support for the enforcement of such general integrity constraints as entity integrity and referential integrity, either explicitly or utilizing a combination of RDBMS features.

■ Entity integrity is enforced by not allowing a primary key to have null values.
■ Referential integrity states that the value of a foreign key must either wholly match the value of the primary key of one of the occurrences of the master entity or that its value is null.

Typically such constraints are defined declaratively in the RDBMS. This has the advantage that the constraint is defined once rather than each time a process has to operate upon the database.

Similarly, application-specific integrity constraints may also be described in some database management systems. A constraint such as: 'A borrower may not borrow further books if the borrower has an outstanding fine' may be specified once in the DBMS and is invoked automatically when a new loan is to be recorded for a borrower. The DBMS not only encompasses the data definition but also the definition of all the rules governing the manipulation of the data.

There are, however, difficulties with this approach. Firstly, the integrity constraints may be too complex to be expressed within the database language. Secondly the automatic features of the DBMS may make it difficult to deal with exceptional cases – once the integrity constraint is enforced it may be enforced without exception.

It is thus important to identify those circumstances when it is appropriate to utilize the more sophisticated features of the implementation environment. As the descriptive power of modern DBMSs increases and their performance continues to improve they will be used to encompass more aspects of the implementation. Rules traditionally specified in programs will increasingly be found in the data definitions.

8.7 Physical process design

This chapter has concentrated so far on physical data design and has commented, in the last section, how functions traditionally dealt with by programs are being shifted across to data design.

However, programs still have to be written for the rules embodied in our Action Diagrams, Update Process Model, Logical Access Map, Enquiry Access Path, Object Life History or State chart (see chapters 6 and 7).

These models specify the logical business requirements. These must be transferred into a physical program design.

In general good programs should be:

- **Functionally correct**. They match the definition provided in the Action Diagram or its equivalent. In our own company the Action Diagram represents the 'contract' between the designer and the programmer. If the program supports the Action Diagram then the programmer has successfully delivered his or her part of the development task.
- **Documented and constructed to the required standard**. Documentation and construction standards will be documented in the Programming and Interface Style Guides. Adherence to these standards will be ensured in walkthroughs and other reviews.
- **Commented**. The Structured English text of the Action Diagram might be integrated into the program structure to provide relevant comments back to the process specification.
- **Tested**. Programs should be tested to agreed standards.
- **Modular.** The last of these deserves consideration. Modularity is concerned with strength and independence. It is vital that modules are as independent as possible so that any change in one module has limited effect on any other modules. This is the issue of *coupling*. Secondly, each module carries out a single problem-related function. This is the issue of *cohesion*.

8.7.1 Coupling

One of the objectives of good design is to minimize coupling. The modules should be as independent as possible. This will ensure that there is less chance of an error being 'rippled' through the system and that the effect of a change in one module has limited effect on other modules. Maintenance and re-coding of one module does not require detailed knowledge of the coding of other modules. A module can be withdrawn and replaced without affecting other modules. Furthermore, the effect of adding new modules to the system is simple and predictable in its effects.

The following types of coupling between modules may be identified:

- **Data coupling**. The exchange of parameters between modules. This is necessary for module control and communication and so is quite harmless as long as the data items are kept to a minimum. It is the 'best' type of coupling.
- **Stamp coupling**. This occurs when a whole data structure is passed to a module and in that structure there are data items that are irrelevant to the called module. Any change in this data structure will affect all modules that use it even if those modules do not refer to the item or items that have been changed. Consequently, stamp coupling introduces dependencies between modules that should be unrelated.
- **Control coupling**. This happens when the calling module passes a flag intended to control the logic of the called module. This has the effect of closely linking

the logic of the two modules. The calling module must know how the called module is organized if it is to send the correct control information. Control flags that tell a module what to do are not permissible. However descriptive flags (Account number is OK) are acceptable because they give information not orders. Control in the hierarchy should be passed through data not flags.

- **Common coupling.** Two modules are common coupled if they refer to the same common data area. These common data areas are defined within the context of the target programming language. In FORTRAN COMMON can be used to declare common areas across SUBROUTINEs and FUNCTIONs. In COBOL, a DATA DIVISION is accessible to any paragraph in the PROCEDURE DIVISION. Common coupling can lead to problems in error rippling, maintenance and inflexibility.

    In such instances the value and meaning of the variables in the data area depend upon the state of the system. In one application known to the authors, the meaning of seven flag data fields depends totally on the programs that are accessing them.

- **Content coupling.** Two modules have content coupling if one module refers to the internal workings of the other. Any changes made to either module will lead to the failure of the other.

Programming Standards should be defined to eliminate unwanted coupling.

8.7.2 Cohesion

This is concerned with examining the internal activities of a single module. In general, one module should perform only one task. Modules that try to perform many tasks – validate input, process data, output results – are difficult to define and maintain. By their very nature their complexity will lead to coupling problems. Hence good coupling should help enforce good cohesion. There are seven forms of cohesion:

- **Functional cohesion.** A module is said to be functionally cohesive when it consists of data items that all contribute to the execution of one task. Such modules are overwhelmingly single-minded. They GET AN EMPLOYEE NAME not print or validate it.
- **Sequential cohesion.** In this instance the activities within the module are related to each other in a way that the output of one activity becomes the input to the next. Thus the module consists of a sequence of actions.
- **Communicational cohesion.** This is a module that performs a number of activities on the same input or output data. For example, the input data Customer Account Number may be used within one module to find Customer Name, Customer Address, Customer Balance, Customer Sex, etc.

    In general Functional, Sequential and Communicational Cohesion are all desirable or acceptable. The latter may create some coupling problems (another module may wish to use Customer Balance) and so a certain amount of vigilance is necessary.

■ **Procedural cohesion**. A procedurally cohesive module is one whose internal activities seem to bear little relationship to each other. The activities in the module may be organized in a sequence but it is *control* rather than *data* that is passed between them. A procedurally cohesive module is usually a bits and pieces module mopping up the activities that have not been catered for elsewhere.

■ **Temporal Cohesion**. These modules are similar to procedurally cohesive modules in that they tend to consist of activities that occur at the same *time*. Their activities are actually more closely related to those in other modules and consequently they often exhibit very 'tight' coupling.

■ **Logical cohesiveness**. A logically cohesive module is one where the selection of activities within the module is dictated from outside. The module contains activities of a general kind, only one of which is selected thorough the common interface. This creates content coupling problems as well as complicating maintenance.

■ **Coincidental cohesiveness**. This occurs in modules with activities that have no logical connection with each other. It is an extreme case of logical cohesiveness. At least the activities of the latter were of the same type. In a coincidentally cohesive module the activities have no temporal, procedural or logical connection. The modules have probably been created by the 'machete method', cutting up longer programs into a 'modularized' design.

8.7.2.1 Size. Modules should not be too large. In the context of commercial programming Page-Jones has suggested that a module might be a:

PROGRAM (or less ideally a SECTION or PARAGRAPH): COBOL
SUBROUTINE or FUNCTION: FORTRAN
FUNCTION: C, APL, PL/1 or ALGOL
PROCEDURE, FUNCTION: ADA or PASCAL

A number of maximum sizes of modules have been suggested (Weinberg, 1971). 'Certainly, all the code of a module should be visible on one page of listing or on two facing pages' (Page-Jones, 1980). This normally sets an upper limit of 120 lines. Myers (1978) has suggested that 'experience has shown that a well-structured program has an average module size of 40–50 high level executable statements (i.e. excluding declarative and comment statements)'.

It is important to recognize that there are no absolute standards, which may lead to arbitrary divisions based on program length rather than considerations of cohesion and coupling. However, it must be acknowledged that many modules (particularly in 4GLs) are much too long for comfort. Functionally limited modules are much easier to program, control and maintain.

8.7.2.2 Re-usable. The issue of re-usability has already been raised in chapter 7. However, on a simpler level it is important to avoid modules that use items whose value has to be taken over from one call to the next. A module should be constructed such that it acts each time like the first occasion on which it was called. It should require no state memory – a figure dependent upon a past existence.

Re-usability is also reduced by hard-coding. The module can only deal with specific values and not any parameter passed to it by the calling module. In contrast, modules are too general when they allow excessive breadth in the passed parameters.

There are many books on program design and the development of Object-oriented Programming Languages (OOPLs) has further fuelled the debate and challenged some of the old concepts. As a noted author has written: 'Re-use is possible in conventional languages, but object-oriented languages greatly enhance the possibility of code re-use' (Rumbaugh *et al.*, 1991). Booch (1994) is particularly concerned with encouraging and *rewarding* re-use so that it becomes the way the department goes about its work: 'Ultimately, any amount of re-use is better than none, because re-use represents a savings of resources that would otherwise be needed to re-invent some previously solved problem'.

8.8 Summary

This chapter has examined some of the issues encountered when moving from the logical design to its equivalent physical design. A number of points must be stressed.

- The logical data design must be adhered to unless performance or software limitations (as in a hierarchical DBMS) dictate otherwise.
- If performance is a problem then a software or hardware solution should be attempted before changing the logical design.
- If the logical design is changed then a map must be created and maintained showing the relationship of physical files and fields to entities and their attributes.
- An increasing number of elements of process definition are now being implemented in the Data Dictionary.

At the end of chapter 6 the reader was invited to evaluate the process models against a number of criteria. You may now like to extend this evaluation to the elements of good program design introduced in the last section. How well do Action Diagrams, Update Process Models, LAMs and EAPs (and any others you wish to consider) promote programs that are:

- functionally correct;
- documented;
- commented;
- not too large;
- modular;
- re-usable;

and, in general, adhere to the standards of the company.

Finally, it must be recognized that some companies make an organizational distinction between logical and physical design. The latter (particularly for data) is left in the hands of the DBA team who are experts in particular software and its performance on a particular machine. Developers are required to produce their data design in Third Normal Form and then leave physical tuning to a small expert team.

9 Systems Controls

9.1 Introduction

Controls have to be implemented in all stages of systems development. They are particularly critical in input design (to prevent Garbage In–Garbage Out) but such operational controls must not be unduly stressed at the cost of those in other phases of system development. This chapter begins by identifying the areas of risk using the 'onion-skin' approach suggested by Wong (1981), which provides a framework for systematically identifying computer-related risks (see figure 9.1). Controls to prevent and detect errors and incursions are presented in subsequent sections of the chapter.

9.2 Areas of risk

Wong's model (see figure 9.1) identifies risks due to:

- **Corporate objectives.** These risks occur where the computer installation is affiliated to a company whose objectives do not command general approval. This may be due to a number of factors such as pollution, warfare contracts, personal injustice or political animosity.
- **Economic factors.** Trade problems and recession may create a number of circumstances that affect the security of the computer department. Economic issues will be important both to the individual (who may be suffering personal money problems) and to the group involved in organized collective bargaining. Precautions will also have to be taken to secure continuity of supply and maintenance.
- **Physical environment.** Typical problems are fire, floods, pollution and explosions. Other risks may include air crashes (if the computer centre is built near an airport), road accidents and vandalism. Wong feels that:

    Of the many problems which threaten the computer operation, those affecting the physical environment are perhaps the easiest to comprehend and for which to organize safeguards.

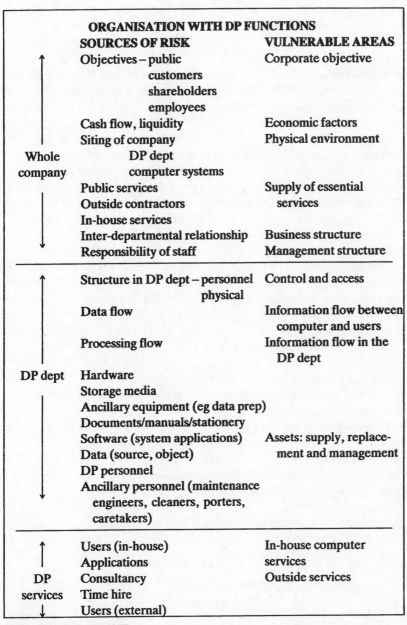

ORGANISATION WITH DP FUNCTIONS	
SOURCES OF RISK	**VULNERABLE AREAS**

Whole company

Objectives – public	Corporate objective
customers	
shareholders	
employees	
Cash flow, liquidity	Economic factors
Siting of company	Physical environment
DP dept	
computer systems	
Public services	Supply of essential
Outside contractors	services
In-house services	
Inter-departmental relationship	Business structure
Responsibility of staff	Management structure

DP dept

Structure in DP dept – personnel	Control and access
physical	
Data flow	Information flow between
	computer and users
Processing flow	Information flow in the
	DP dept
Hardware	
Storage media	
Ancillary equipment (eg data prep)	
Documents/manuals/stationery	
Software (system applications)	Assets: supply, replace-
Data (source, object)	ment and management
DP personnel	
Ancillary personnel (maintenance	
engineers, cleaners, porters,	
caretakers)	

DP services

Users (in-house)	In-house computer
Applications	services
Consultancy	Outside services
Time hire	
Users (external)	

Source: K K Wong, 1977

Figure 9.1 The 'onion skin' approach to the systematic identification of computer related risks.

■ **Supply of essential services.** Essential services include water, heat, gas, and most crucially, power. Loss of these facilities may either be deliberate (due to an industrial dispute) or accidental (a dog chewing through a power cable). Whatever the reason a back-up generator is essential if computer operations must continue. Security problems may also result from breakdown of communication lines or wire tapping.

■ **Business structure.** This will encompass fraud, industrial action and boycotts by user departments. It will also include circumstances where the management structure too easily permits fraudulent activity that can be blamed on 'computer errors'.

A large number of fraud cases are permitted, perhaps encouraged, by lack of attention to management reporting structures. Careful consideration of organizational arrangements is essential. Adequate reporting and auditing controls must be established in a structure that recognizes a proper segregation of duties.

The risks identified so far are relevant to the whole company. However, there are also significant security problems within the information systems section itself. These may arise from:

■ **Staff relations.** Wong states that 'Demotivated staff are unlikely to obtain satisfaction from their jobs, and may well believe that they are inadequately rewarded or receive insufficient praise for their efforts...'. This may lead them in to temptation, attempting to by-pass the security system either as a challenge, or for financial gain.

■ **Information flow.** This encompasses flow of data from the data processing department to the user and also within the computer section itself. This will include the disclosure or misuse of confidential information, perhaps for blackmail, by users and data processing staff acting in collusion. Risks within the data processing department include negligence, accidents and a lack of discipline in the development of systems.

■ **Risks arising from the supply, replacement and management of computer resources.** Wong includes the following risks in this category:
  – faulty equipment, stationery and software;
  – breakdown of hardware, software and systems;
  – arson, theft and sabotage;
  – business interruption;
  – misplacement or destruction of data, programs, etc.;
  – out-of-date program and system documentation;
  – sickness and injury to senior staff;
  – industrial action and blackmail;
  – misappropriation of computer resources;
  – data corruption and decay of storage media.

■ **Risks from supplying or receiving computer services.** These arise from the moral and legal liabilities associated with offering services to both internal and external users. Such risks are particularly significant in offering services to external customers. Thus organizations selling information services might have the following problems:

– mis-routing of output;
– poor delivery of services;
– liabilities associated with late delivery and/or poor performance
– contractual risks;
– staff misconduct;
– professional errors and omissions on consultancy assignments.

Thus security risks occur at a number of levels and the current extent of computer fraud is difficult to quantify. Some commentators feel that it is underestimated while others believe that the whole problem is inflated out of its true proportion. Norman (1981) comments that:

> The vast majority of all computer insecurity incidents can be traced back to application programs. Most computer goofs are application program errors, either in program specification or writing. Most reported 'computer fraud' has been achieved either by writing (rarely) fraudulent programs or by exploiting (commonly) loopholes deliberately or accidently left in programs.
>
> (Norman, 1981)

Developing software controls that identify errors and unauthorized access is an important task and such controls are examined in detail in the following section. However, having acknowledged this, it must also be stated that many lapses of physical security have also been recorded. Norman lists a catalogue of incidents identified by Lewis Security Systems. Three examples are listed below and they serve to demonstrate that computer security is perhaps not taken as seriously as it should be.

Case 1
The report of an open side door to a secure computer centre. This was used to pop outside for fresh air, although 'we are air-conditioned'.

Case 2
The case of an alert guard who noticed a visitor wearing the wrongly coloured badge, stopped the man, and immediately issued him with the correctly coloured badge for that area, without any interrogation.

Case 3
The computer complex with three computer halls protected by eleven locked doors each with a card lock. All eleven locks were jammed or distorted but 'we have not had them repaired because the large number of temporary staff on shifts would necessitate our issuing them all with cards'.

9.3 Systems controls

In practice most documented software errors are caused by accident; the wrong input of data, incorrectly defined processing, misinterpreted output. These are due to genuine mistakes, mis-keying and misunderstandings. It is the tasks of the system developer to design systems that minimize the chance of such errors reaching processing or system outputs. Controls will be required on data at all stages of its collection, processing, storage and retrieval. Data should be accurate and complete at all times, and its manipulation both authorized and legitimate. It is important to recognize that the necessary controls will be implemented in the clerical procedures of the system as well as in the software itself.

9.3.1 Clerical controls

It may be possible to implement control totals that are summed both manually and automatically. These totals are compared and if they agree than the data is assumed to have been entered correctly and the batch can be posted for processing. Such totals are particularly common in accounting systems where the accuracy of data is paramount. Addition may be on inappropriate fields such as account numbers and the nominal codes entered on the batch. These are useful accuracy checks but clearly they have no particular significance. These meaningless sums are often termed hash totals.

Clerical controls are also of importance where source documents are posted around sections or buildings. It is very easy for forms or returns to be lost in transit with the result that certain transactions, such as employee payments, do not take place. Movement control is usually enforced by the completion of batch control documents that give sufficient information for the recipient to check for the completeness of contents. Typical of data on a control sheet would be:

- **Serial number of the batch**. To check whether this follows the last received batch of documents. Has a whole batch gone missing in the post?
- **Count of batch contents**. The number of forms that should be in the batch.
- **Serial numbers of forms**. The serial numbers or number range(s) of the enclosed forms.

Such checks will be a part of the input system described in chapter 2. A large information systems centre will have a section dedicated to data control, responsible for checking input data, enforcing input schedules, locating errors, organizing and validating output, etc. They will also wish to impose standards of good housekeeping so that disks are properly and clearly labelled, unused files deleted, proper control documentation established and maintained. This is often sadly missing in personal computer (PC) installations where disks go unlabelled (or labels never changed), hard disks become cluttered with obliquely named files that no one can recall creating, let alone naming, and backup procedures ignored because 'we haven't got enough spare disks'.

9.3.2 Software controls

The source for most of these checks will be a data element Data Dictionary definition. These will permit the formulation of a whole range of controls performed by the software itself. Thus the system is used to trap input errors using the skill and knowledge of the system's developer. Typical of these checks are:

■ **Format checks.** This is to check that data always conforms to the specified format. Thus a product code designated as two letters followed by four numbers is always entered this way. Invalid entries such as A2341 or AS231 are rejected.

■ **Range checks.** The data has to lie within certain values. These may be set globally (e.g. Property Reference Code must be between 100 and 200) or may be more selective to identify uncommon occurrences. Thus, if 90 per cent of all Property Reference Codes are between 100 and 110, then legitimate, but infrequent codes may trigger a request for operator checking: 'You have entered code 121. This is a Warehouse. Please confirm that this code is correct...'.

■ **Sequence checks.** Used to test that transactions that are supposed to be in a certain order are actually arranged this way. Thomas and Douglas (1981) comment that:

> Although well-known, this check is not applied in systems as widely as it could be. Coupled with the issue of sequentially prenumbered stationery, where stationery control is exercised, this check can provide control over a number of aspects of the non-computer part of the system.

■ **Consistency checks.** Two data items may be related in some way. Thus 'maternity leave' is always associated with sex = 'female'. Many such relationships exist and should be exploited to the full. It should stop some of the more ludicrous errors like those quoted in Warner and Stone of one air*man* discharged on the grounds of pregnancy, and the award of a flying badge to a carpenter (Warner and Stone, 1970).

■ **Record and item counts.** Counting the items (how many invoices that have been entered) represents a simpler but less reliable alternative to control and hash totals.

■ **Flag fields.** The inclusion of flag fields that record whether a certain state or process has taken place. These are essentially included in the file definition for control purposes only. Thus if a salary field has been updated the flag is set to a value that traps all subsequent attempts to access the salary information. It can be viewed as a switch that is set once and prevents any subsequent activity until it is reset.

■ **Code design.** It may be feasible to implement a code design that has elements of self-checking. Thus the first facet of the code (say the first three numbers) may be split off and certain checks performed. Included, among these might be consistency checks against other parts of the code: 'If the first three numbers of the code are less than 100 check that the fourth number is not greater than 7.' This code was part of one used for supply requisitioning. The first three numbers were employee codes. Those with a code beginning with less than 100 could not order more than £7(000) worth of goods.

A code is helped by the addition of a check digit. This represents a number added to the end of the code that permits the rest of the code to be checked for transcription, transposition and random errors. One of the most common methods of allocating a check digit is the modulus 11 algorithm. This is best illustrated by example:

A company uses product numbers of six digits: 345213 is a typical example. It wishes to incorporate a check digit into the code in an attempt to reduce the number of clerical input errors. This will thus make a new seven digit code.

The method of calculation is as follows:

Number		3	4	5	2	1	3
Multiplier		6	5	4	3	2	1
Product		18	20	20	6	2	3
Sum of Products	69						
Divide by modulus 11		6 remainder 3					

The remainder is added to the code to make the new one:
   3452133

Everytime that this code is entered by the operator the software undertakes a modulus 11 check to validate the check digit. If the last entered figure is 3 and the rest of the code is correct then the input is permitted. The value of this can be demonstrated by the effect of a simple transposition error.

Number		3	5	4	2	1	3	3
Multiplier		6	5	4	3	2	1	
Product		18	25	16	6	2	3	
Sum of products	70							
Divide by modulus 11		6 remainder 4						

The check digit is incorrect and so an error has been made in the entry.

It should be recognized that all these checks should be applied together. The erroneous input 3542133 may have survived format and range checks only to be tripped up by the check digit. However, the latter is not a coding panacea. Thomas and Douglas point out that it will not prevent the mistake of a user who has a list of valid and verifiable numbers and applies the wrong one by mistake. They suggest that 'a check digit system always has some value, but the auditor should assess how much reliance should be placed on it' (Thomas and Douglas, 1981).

9.3.3 Procedure control

Most documents in business systems are related in some way. For example, an order normally precedes an invoice, an invoice precedes a credit note, an invoice precedes a receipt. In some circumstances the modification of one document is prescribed by law or policy. So, for example, an invoice sent to a customer and recorded in the sales ledger may not be subsequently altered and reissued. If the content of the invoice is wrong, then the correct procedure is to send a credit note for all or part of that amount. These controls must be integrated into the systems design. For example, the amend facility on the Invoice data entry screen must be disabled after confirmation of invoice despatch.

Some elements of control will emerge from the Entity Life History and the dialogue design. However, it is also possible to use state charts (State transition diagrams) and decision tables for more complex circumstances. The order form example in chapter 7 demonstrates the control modelling of a state chart and its effective expression of the business rules that apply in a particular enterprise.

9.3.4 Dialogue controls

Martin (1973), in his consideration of accuracy controls in real-time systems suggests that transaction checks naturally become more significant because batches do not exist. He places great emphasis on the role of interface design in reducing erroneous entries, providing 'eight vital aspects' in the 'battle for accuracy on real-time systems':

1: The psychological considerations in dialogue design must be planned so as to minimize the probability of terminal operator errors.
2: The dialogue must be structured in such a way as to catch as many errors as possible, immediately.
3: The system must be planned so as to facilitate immediate correction of errors caught.
4: The real-time error-detection process must be backed up with off-line file inspection and, if applicable, balancing routines.
5: Self-checking operations must be built into both the real-time dialogue and the linkage of this dialogue to the file-inspection routines.
6: Transactions and posting procedures must be devised so that transaction balances and file balances can be taken where they are useful.
7: Procedures must be worked out to bridge all periods of system failure and recovery in such a way that errors are not introduced here.
8: Careful controls must be devised to prevent unauthorised persons from modifying the files or making entries at terminals.

This list is significant for two main reasons:

■ It recognizes the importance of dialogue design almost a decade before it became fashionable. The growth of on-line systems has led to the interface becoming much more important and hence the developer should be at ease with different interface types and principles of good practice (see chapters 2 and 3). It has become a major weapon in error detection.
■ The list demonstrates the interaction of interface, input and control design. These three facets should reinforce each other. A well-designed screen is devalued if it permits the entry of erroneous data, while validated data items on a friendly screen are reduced in impact if they are irrelevant or incomplete.

9.4 The auditing function

In many organizations the internal auditor makes an important contribution to systems development. It is important that the systems developer understands the work of audit and how auditors go about their work.

9.4.1 The scope of audit

Audit may encompass:

- **Examining and reviewing the organizational and operational controls of the computer department.** This covers an overall review of general principles, management and organization. Tasks might include:
  - an investigation into how system developments are established, controlled and resourced;
  - a review of whether there are adequate controls and division of duties in the specification, development, testing and incorporation of program amendments;
  - an inspection of operating logs to see if they are properly maintained, scrutinized and filed.
- **Reviewing application systems which are under development or being run.** This will consist of a general review of each separate application or procedure. Tasks might include:
  - A consideration of the feasibility study report to see whether it meets the defined terms of reference.
  - An inspection of the development timetable to see whether it is realistic and fits in with corporate plans.
  - An evaluation of the planned training strategy to see whether it is both reasonable and realistic.
- **Providing controls in systems specification and development.** The auditor should be able to both participate in and evaluate critically the specification models produced in the project. It is essential that audit is considered at every stage of the system development cycle and not just tagged on at the end as a series of operational controls. Such participation will ensure that checks are both relevant and timely. It should also mean that the auditor has a detailed and complete picture of the system that has been built up over a long period of time. The task of auditing a system 'cold' is really quite daunting. Tasks might include:
  - A review of the terms of reference to see if they are unambiguous and adequate for the task at hand. Sloppily defined terms of reference can lead to project difficulties and disagreements between the parties involved.
  - Checking the existence and quality of models such as the Data Flow Diagram and the Logical Data Structure. Ensuring that, where appropriate, user sign-offs have been agreed and recorded.
  - Check program code and adherence to program standards.
  - Ensure that all manuals are complete, up to date, and relevant to the users or operators that they are intended for.
  - Ensure that systems have been tested properly and in accordance with defined standards.
- **Carry out efficiency and effectiveness audits.** Tasks might include:
  - An inspection of system costings and the method adopted to 'charge' these costs out to users. An assessment of the principle and fairness of such charging arrangements.
  - Auditing live systems to ensure that data is being processed properly and fairly.

Thus auditing has a wide scope and is not purely concerned with compliance to established accounting and financial procedures. This range of activity may not be recognized by the organization, or indeed by the auditor's themselves:

> auditing has been linked with the accounting function, and on the whole has not extended its scope to become interested in compliance or security within the data processing area.
> (Chambers, 1986)

9.4.2 Auditing techniques

The detailed auditing techniques available to the auditor include the following.

9.4.2.1 Test data method. In this method, the auditor prepares some dummy data and passes it through the system. The affect of this data is predicted in advance: how it will be presented in reports, the effect of processes on it, which data items should be rejected or questioned, etc. These predictions are then compared with the results from the system run and any discrepancies are investigated. In many respects it is like the system testing (see chapter 10), but in this instance it is undertaken by an external observer – an auditor and not the system developer.

Test data must be carefully controlled within the system, so that legitimate transactions are not sparked off by them. There are many, perhaps apocryphal stories, of vanloads of goods touring the European mainland looking for fictitious addresses entered by auditors as part of the test data. In such instances the dummy nature of the data had not been recognized and as a result the usual administrative arrangements had been set in motion.

This latter problem can be overcome by establishing areas of the system that are specifically for audit testing purposes. Thus a firm may set up a customer, a department or an account specifically allocated to audit. This section of the system works like all the rest but the usual physical consequences of the processing are withheld. This integrated test facility is usually feasible where the system has been designed with audit as one of its main design objectives. The weakness of this approach is ensuring that the dummy audit sections are actually working the same as the rest of the system and have not been singled out for special, legitimate processing!

Chambers (1986) states that the test data method may be used to good effect in the following circumstances:

- to test input data controls, including data validation;
- to test processing logic and controls;
- to test computation of such values as discounts, payslips, VAT and commission;
- to test related manual controls.

He feels that it is a useful audit tool but that it is very time consuming and only gives a snapshot of the system's activities. It only deals with dummy data and so 'it cannot be said to directly contribute to the verification of balance sheet and operating statement items, or any other items'. The external auditor will be more concerned with verification and so he is more interested in an auditing technique that permits him to interrogate real data. This will not only give the verification he requires but also provide an insight into the system's controls. Direct access is provided by Audit Enquiry programs.

9.4.2.2 Audit enquiry programs. These packages vary widely in sophistication but they are primarily used to examine files, retrieve data and produce requested reports. They permit the auditor to access the system files and data directly and to make the required tests and enquiries on the actual operational figures. Chambers feels that such packages help the auditor in five ways.

1: They compensate for the loss of visual evidence. The records may be read almost as if they were their physical equivalents.
2: Data may be extracted for further audit investigation. Thus problems and inconsistencies may be pursued through subsequent enquiries. In this way the audit enquiry program is a much more sensitive tool than the test data approach.
3: They provide independent verification of the values, details and analysis of the presented data. The test data method cannot do this because it cannot use the real figures.
4: Complex calculations may be conducted faster, more accurately and more completely than with clerical audit procedures.
5: 'They allow identification of items which do not comply with the laid down system rules or which, while complying, seem unreasonable.'

9.4.2.3 The operating system. The Operating System may be a useful source of audit information. Most Operating Systems maintain operational logs that record what use has been made of the system. In many practical instances it has been the Operating System that has provided important clues about fraudulent activity. Pointers have included statistics about use, aborted attempts to log into certain files, high activity on files at unusual times and overuse of certain terminals.

In a useful review of the audit facilities of a selection of mainframe Operating Systems (Douglas, 1983) Sandra Bennett describes the Burroughs System Log and lists the utilities that are available to interrogate it. These include an 'analyser' that can print all or part of either the current or previous logs:

The utility provides facilities for printing information relating to periods of time, particular jobs or particular types of messages. One of these options will print a list of security violations. Another option will provide information on hardware faults...

(Norman, 1983)

Many Operating System developers have tried to offer flexibility in their software by giving more optional security facilities. These are useful when the computer section know they exist, know how to use them and, as importantly, know when to use them However, such flexibility can lead to more opportunity for fraudulent activity. Bennett, in her review of the Burroughs Master Control Program (MCP) reveals that:

It is possible to compile and run the MCP with both the system log and the job log required options set off. Burroughs do not recommend this, but it is possible.

(Douglas, 1983)

Mainframe computers maintain detailed logs as a matter of course (unless they are turned off!) and have often provided the information required to trap unauthorized activity. Personal computers usually have very rudimentary logging facilities, if any at all! The log might only detail the name of the file, it size and the date and time that it was last accessed. One suggestion is that 'a manual log be maintained in an agreed form. The auditor should review the type of logging system in operation, and should carry out random checks on the log to ensure that programs were run as scheduled, and they only accessed permitted files' (Thomas and Douglas, 1981). This may appear good sense but it does appear rather optimistic. It is unusual for many users to know what files are on a disk, let alone details of the last amendments and updates. The security and audit shortcomings of personal computer Operating Systems are likely to continue reducing the chance of performing an effective system audit.

9.4.3 Audit trail

The audit trail is designed in conjunction with the internal auditor. The trail will record significant data about each transaction. Audit trails are particularly significant in PC software where the Operating System cannot be relied upon to give any valuable audit information.

9.5 Legal requirements: Data protection legislation

A number of attempts were made to introduce Data Protection legislation in the 1960s. These were mainly Private Member's Bills and stood little chance of reaching the Statute Book. In 1970 an official Committee, under the chairmanship of Kenneth Younger, was established to consider privacy intrusions. However, they were restricted to examining the private sector, a limit that caused some concern.

The Younger Committee made a series of recommendations and the Government reacted to these by producing a White Paper on the subject in 1975 – three and a half years after the Younger Commission had reported! This paper also established a Data Protection Committee to advise the Government on legislative requirements. The Chairman was Sir Norman Lindop and his committee reported in December 1978. His work was largely lost in the change of government in 1979 (from Labour to Conservative) and the subsequent White Paper of 1982 did not borrow many of its principles. The Data Protection Authority proposed by the Lindop Committee was replaced by a Registrar appointed by the Crown. Similarly, statutory codes of practice favoured by Lindop, were rejected as impractical as they would impose 'an unacceptable burden on resources'. It was the 1982 paper that formed the basis of the subsequent Data Protection Bill.

9.5.1 Data Protection Act, 1984

The Data Protection Act received its Royal Assent on the 12 July 1984. It applies to automatically processed personal data, giving rights to individuals to access data held about them and to seek compensation for loss or damage caused by the misuse of personal data. The Act is enforced by the Data Protection Registrar. The Act uses a number of definitions:

- **Data**. This means information recorded in a form in which it can be processed by equipment operating automatically in response to instructions given for that purpose.
- **Personal Data**. This means data consisting of information that relates to a living individual who can be identified from that information, including any expression of opinion about the individual but not any indication of the intentions of the Data User in respect of that individual.

The word 'automatic' is important. The Bill excludes manual records. In some respects this could be interpreted as an incentive to de-computerize sensitive information. For example, coded records that identify individuals could be maintained on a system where one field is used to point to a manual file reference containing controversial statements. Data subjects would have access to the computer held data but not (under the terms of the Act) to the manual data to which the computer system refers. The absence of a complementary Freedom of Information Act permits the exploitation of this loophole:

- **Data Subject**. This means an individual who is the subject of personal data.
- **Data User**. This means a person who holds data and/or controls the contents and use of the data. A Data User is able to register details of their data with the Data Protection Registrar and to have these placed on the Data Protection Register.

A Data Subject is, given certain exemptions and conditions, able to examine what personal data is being held about him or her by the Data User. The subject may then ask for a copy of such data.

9.5.1.1 Principles. The Data Protection Act, 1984 is framed within the spirit of the following principles:

- The information to be contained in personal data shall be obtained, and personal data shall be processed, fairly and lawfully.

Persons providing information should not be mislead about the purposes for which the data will be used.

- Personal data shall be held only for one or more specified and lawful purposes. These specific purposes are listed on the Register.
- Personal data held for any purpose or purposes shall not be used or disclosed in any manner incompatible with that purpose or those purposes.
- Personal data held for any purpose or purposes shall be adequate, relevant and not excessive in relation to that purpose or those purposes.

The role of the Data Dictionary in reinforcing this principle is worth stressing. The compilation of the dictionary should ensure that the role of every data item in the system can be explained and justified.

■ Personal data shall be accurate and, where necessary, kept up to date.

Where accurate means correct and not misleading as to any matter of fact. Personal data received from a third party is viewed as accurate if both of the following conditions apply:

- The data and any information extracted from it are marked as received data.
- If the individual the data relates to has told the user that he or she considers the data to be inaccurate, then this has been recorded with the data.
- These facts are displayed on all screen displays and printouts.

The design implications of these requirements requires some thought. It appears necessary to add two fields to many systems, one denoting the source of the data and, if it is received, another acknowledging the accuracy of that data from the Data Subject. The designer must also decide what is meant by 'up to date' in the context of the accuracy of a particular data item.

■ Personal data held for any purpose or purposes shall not be kept for longer than is necessary for that purpose or purposes.
■ An individual shall be entitled: At reasonable intervals and without undue delay or expense to:
- be informed by any Data User whether he or she holds personal data of which that individual is the Subject; and
- to access any such data held by a Data User; and, where appropriate, to have such data corrected or erased.

Thus the Data Subject becomes, in effect, another user of the system whose requirements must be taken into consideration in design. The data user must respond to a subject access request within 40 days of receiving it:

■ Appropriate security measures shall be taken against unauthorized access to, or alteration, disclosure or destruction of, personal data and against accidental loss or destruction of personal data.

9.5.1.2 Rights of individuals. The Data Subject has right of access to data held about him or herself. This is in accordance with one of the principles of Data Protection and is laid down in detail in the Act itself. An individual shall be entitled to:

- be informed by any Data User whether the data held by him include personal data of which that individual is a Data Subject; and
- to be supplied by any Data User with a copy of the information constituting any such personal data held by him.

The request from the Data Subject for such information must be made in writing and be accompanied by the required fee.

The Courts may order Data Users to pay compensation for damage suffered by Data Users as a result of:

- loss of data;
- destruction of data without the authority of the Data User;
- disclosure of, or access to, data without the authority of the Data User;
- inaccurate data.

Claims for compensation must concern financial or physical damage: although if a subject is awarded compensation for such damage the court may also award additional compensation for distress suffered (Hook, 1989).

9.5.1.3 Exemptions. The Data Subject does not have rights of access to the data if it is held for certain circumstances or for certain purposes or reasons. Briefly, these are:

- data held for:
  - 'the prevention or detection of crime'
  - 'the apprehension or prosecution of offenders'
  - 'the assessment or collection of any tax or duty'.
- data held by a government department, supplied by a third party, in connection with the making of judicial appointments; (this covers the appointment of judges but not of jurors).
- data to which legal professional privilege (as between lawyer and client) could be claimed;
- data held solely for statistical or research purposes. This is on condition that the data is not used for any other purpose and that results do not identify particular data subjects;
- data whose disclosure is prohibited by law where the Secretary of State decides that this prohibition should override the subject access provisions in the interests of the Data Subject or any other individual and makes an order conferring exemption;
- data covered by the Consumer Credit, Act 1974;
- data held solely for recovery or 'back up';
- data held by regulatory bodies discharging statutory functions in connection with the protection of the public against dishonesty, incompetence or malpractice in financial matters;

The Secretary of State may also make Orders exempting from the subject access provisions or modifying these provisions in relation to:

- data concerning physical or mental health or social work.

The exemptions above apply to *subject access*. Certain systems are excluded from the act *as a whole*. These include:

- Personal data that are required to be exempt for the purpose of safeguarding national security. A certificate is required to support the exemption signed by a Cabinet Minister, the Attorney General or the Lord Advocate.
- Personal data held for the purposes of payroll, pensions or accounts.
- Data held by an individual 'concerned only with the management of his personal, family or household affairs or held by him only for recreational purposes'.

- Data held by an unincorporated members' club and relating only to members.
- Data consisting only of names and addresses and used only for the distribution of articles or information.

Neither of the preceding two exemptions applies unless the data subject has been asked whether he or she objects to the personal data being held, and has not objected. The exemption for distribution lists only applies if the system consists only of data items necessary for distribution. The exemption is lost if more than just name and address is held.

9.5.1.4 *Design implications of the Act.*

- **Survey and registration.** An initial survey of applications must be undertaken, establishing whether registration is necessary and, if it is, producing the information required for registration. This may be a large undertaking, particularly identifying applications developed on personal computers outside of the control of data processing management. This survey must also determine whether the standards and procedures of applications are rigorous enough to comply with the requirements of the Act.
- **Ensuring continuous compliance with the Act.** Applications must remain within their stated scope. New applications and extensions and maintenance to current systems must be investigated and, if necessary, registered. It is a criminal offence to operate outside of the terms of the register entry. Furthermore, each register entry is only for a maximum of 3 years. It must be renewed within 6 months of the date that it is due to expire. Failure to renew an entry will require a fresh application for registration.
- **Ensuring security.** One of the Data Protection principles explicitly recognises the necessity of appropriate security measures against unauthorised access to, or alteration, disclosure or destruction of, personal data and against accidental loss or destruction of personal data.
- **Responding to requests for information.** Developing administrative procedures, controls and enquiry routines for data subjects. The data subject becomes another user of the system and this should be reflected in system design. A system will have to be established for administering subject accesses and the costs and fees for such an access.
- **Clerical procedures.** Ensuring that correct clerical procedures support the computer applications.

Staff at all levels in an organization play an important role in ensuring the organization's compliance with the legislation. They may be personally liable for offences committed under the Act, as well as responsible for committing the organization.

(Peat, Marwick, 1984)

- **Software design.** Extra data fields may be required to fulfil the requirements of the Act. For example, to resist a charge of holding incorrect data you have to indicate whether the data was supplied by the data subject or by a third party. Computer files will have to be extended and amended to include that indicator.

9.5.2 Computer Misuse Act, 1990

The Computer Misuse Act received its Royal Assent on the 29 June 1990. It came into force on the 29 August 1990 and, from that date, it became a criminal offence for anyone to (or attempt to) access or modify computer held data or software without authority to do so. The Act was largely created to deal with computer hacking, viruses and other nuisances that did not fit easily into previous legislation.

The Act introduces powers to prosecute those who deliberately misuse computer systems belonging to their employers or third parties. Unlike the Data Protection Act there is no restriction in the type of data or application covered by the Act. Furthermore, there is no supervisory body, such as a Registrar, to enforce the legislation. Like most criminal offences, the enforcement of this Act is the responsibility of the police.

The Act defines three offences;

- A person is guilty of an Unauthorized Access Offence if:
  - he or she causes a computer to perform any function with intent to secure access to any program or data held in any computer;
  - the access he or she intends to secure is unauthorized; and
  - he or she knows at the time that he causes the function that that is the case.

Although this offence is partly aimed at hacking, its wording means that it also applies to internal authorized users who attempt to gain access to parts of the system to which they are officially denied access. It is estimated that 70–80 per cent of unauthorized access is carried out by insiders (Elbra, 1990). A person accused of this offence alone would be tried in a Magistrates' or Sheriff's court and face a fine up to £2,000 and/or imprisonment for up to 6 months. This offence is primarily aimed at those who wish to explore the system for amusement and nuisance value. Successfully gaining access to the system is reward in itself. The interloper has no interest in changing the data or using it for further gain.

- The second offence (the Ulterior Intent Offence), is concerned with unauthorized access that leads to a serious crime. In this case the accused has the intention of using the information (for example, debt position or sexual proclivity) to commit further offences – such as fraud or blackmail. This offence has a maximum prison sentence of 5 years and/or an unlimited fine.
- The final offence is the Unauthorized Modification Offence. A person is guilty of this offence if:
  - he does any act which causes an unauthorized modification of the contents of any computer; and
  - at the time when he does the act he has the requisite intent and the requisite knowledge.

The requisite intent is an attempt to cause a modification of the contents of any computer and by so doing:

- to impair the operation of any computer;

– to prevent or hinder access to any program or data held in any computer: or

– to impair the operation of any such program or the reliability of any such data.

In this case the interloper has changed the data in some way to affect the operation and reliability of the data. For example, a credit limit might be changed, an overdraft position deleted or an examination mark amended. The penalty for this offence is up to 5 years in prison and/or an unlimited fine.

Elbra argues that alterations to the software caused by Trojan Horses, logic bombs or viruses will be covered by this offence. The producer of the virus commits this offence even though he or she does not know in advance which computers will be affected.

9.5.2.1 Design implications of the Act.

■ **Prevention**. Unlike the Data Protection Act,1984 there is no legal requirement for an enterprise to establish any particular level of security or to instigate new administrative or software procedures. Hence, there is no obligation placed on the computer user. They can ignore the Act if they wish. However, it is clearly in the interest of the company to protect itself from the offences identified in the Act.

Prevention will include the implementation of physical security procedures. Restricting access to hardware and software will lessen the chance of misuse by staff and outsiders.

■ **Access rights for users must be clearly understood and specified**. The Data Dictionary will be a useful tool here. The importance and significance of access restrictions must clearly be understood by all staff. Many employees appear to believe that the very fact of their employment gives them access to all areas of the company's systems. 'This belief can only be countered by the issue of a policy statement, supported by standards and procedures, laying down exactly what each end-user is permitted to access and to change, and who is authorized to give that permission' (Elbra, 1990). The absence of such a statement will make prosecution very difficult.

Passwords must be changed at regular intervals and difficult to guess. The control of system 'log-in' also requires attention. Every user must be positively identified before being given access to the software. The more times the user is asked for identification and confirmation, the more barriers are presented to the interloper. It also makes it more difficult for him or her to claim that they were unaware that the access was unauthorized.

■ **Detection**. Unauthorized access will be spotted on the systems log. This obviously does not provide the identification of the interloper. However, the police may then interview the rightful user with the aim of identifying certain suspects.

It is also important to collect and protect evidence of the offence. Elbra suggests that two full copies of the system prior to and after the event must be kept, marked, sealed and secure in conditions in which they will not deteriorate.

It must be stressed that the systems designer is only concerned with allowing the detection of access and the recording of evidence that will withstand cross examination in a Court of Law. The investigation of suspects and prosecution of offenders is the responsibility of the police and the legal profession.

On 11 January 1995 *The Times* reported that a man from Plymouth had become the first person to be charged under this Act. He was accused of spreading two computer viruses; 'Pathogen' and 'Queeg' after a 9 month investigation by police.

9.6 Summary

Controls are required at all stages of development, from initial system definition (is it a correct use of the organization's resources?) to system maintenance (is program documentation amended?, do the changes affect the Data Protection registration?). This chapter has tried to give a wide-ranging review of the types of controls required in systems development. It has particularly considered the legal obligations of designers in the context of two major legislative Acts. The role of internal audit must also be reviewed. In the future, who will check that development has progressed properly and that models fulfil required standards?

10 System Implementation

10.1 Introduction

This chapter examines two aspects of implementation. The first is the practical tasks that have to be completed – testing, conversion, documentation and training. The second is a consideration of the different implementation strategies that can be adopted – pilot implementation, parallel running and direct changeover.

10.2 Testing

During the programming stage each programmer or programming team will perform their own program testing to the specifications laid down by the designer. The completed programs are then passed to the designer for further testing. Testing will be performed by both *desk checking* the program designs with the original specification, and by running the final programs using *test data*.

Test data should be manually compiled and the results produced by the system compared with the appropriate clerical figures or the current computer system. So, for example, in a system designed to produce and print examination certificates, a sample of students should be taken and entered into the new computer system. The certificates can then be compared with their clerically produced counterparts and discrepancies investigated.

It is also important that the system correctly identifies errors and omissions and testing for these is especially critical. Common error tests include the input of:

- oversize and undersize items;
- incorrect formats;
- out of range items;
- no data at all;
- invalid combinations;
- negative numbers.

Outputs also have to be validated, particularly those which are a little unusual, such as the nil Statement and the multi-page Invoice. Testing is a vital but time consuming activity. It is inevitable that errors will be found. These may be due to incorrect programming, misunderstanding of specifications or simply omissions in the original design. The amendments required must be coded by the programmer and the programs and system retested. This retesting is very important because the requested amendments may have caused unwanted side effects and so new errors and problems may appear. One of the most common source of faults in programs is the fixing of other faults!

It is also at the system testing stage that the timing aspects of the system become clearer. Required response times (maximum of 10 seconds for retrieval of patient data), processing times (all employee records updated in 2 hours) and output schedules (all examination certificates produced in a week) must all be checked. Problems that are due to inefficient programming or mis-specified files may be tackled by the designer. This may mean a return to the design model for file restructuring, or the use of faster programming languages in certain modules. Problems due to hardware not achieving its claimed specification must be taken up with the supplier.

A progressive approach to testing might involve:

- **Unit testing.** The validation of the internal code of a program may involve:
  - **Desk checking.** A manual 'walkthrough' of the program checking code against the requirements specification (such as the Action Diagram). This walkthrough will also be concerned with checking that standards have been adhered to as well as identifying opportunities for syntactical and structural improvements.
  - **Compile.** A clean compilation is required.
  - **Test data.** Once the module is known to work then it must be checked to see if it works properly. Test plans are prepared and test results compared with predicted results.
  - **Testing the interfaces between tested programs.** Individual programs may work but they may not work together. Each program is tested with the programs from which it receives and passes data.
- **Integration testing.** This is concerned with validating the operations of a suite of interconnected programs. It seeks to test that a logical sub-system is working correctly and that data is passed properly between the parts of the sub-system.
- **System testing.** This is designed to ensure that the sub-systems work properly together. Such testing is performed against specification and should pass through the following phases:
  - **Single run.** This is testing the system over a single pass of test data.
  - **Cyclic tests.** This involves testing the system over several cycles of processing. This is to ensure that it correctly deals with end-of-day, end-of-month and end-of-year routines.
  - **Volume tests.** Up to this point the minimum set of test data has been used. This must now be extended to examine how the system copes with agreed volumes and possible overloads.

– **Clerical tests**. This involves testing all aspects of the interface between the user and the system.

■ **User acceptance testing**. This is organized and performed by the users. It is concerned with proving, to their satisfaction, that the delivered system meets the specification.

Testing is a time-consuming activity. The use of automated aids to assist the production of test data (e.g. from a Data Dictionary) and for detecting program errors is obviously very useful. If automation extends to program development then a rigorous method of constructing specifications should ensure bug-free programs.

It must be recognized that testing represents the last opportunity for preparing the system modules before their exposure to users and the harshness of the real world. From now on any errors or idiosyncrasies will become public knowledge.

10.3 File conversion

Most systems require an established set of files if they are to be immediately operational. Thus an order entry system will need such files as customer data, outstanding orders, products, etc. This may demand a large file conversion task (when moving from one computer system to another) or a large, one-off data entry when systems are being computerized for the first time. This conversion leads to both programming and management tasks.

If the files are currently held on a computer system then it should be possible to move the data from the present implementation to the target hardware and software. There are many companies that offer this service although both cost and compatibility should be thoroughly investigated. It may also be necessary to write certain routines, such as stripping off control characters or truncating fields to modify the data format after conversion. The mapping of the data items from the current file structures to the target ones must be carefully investigated and documented. The programs that carry out the conversion also have to be tested and the results of test runs on the transfer have to be meticulously checked.

Data entry programs will also have to be written for data that is to be collected for the first time. The designer may be able to use the data input routines of the proposed system for entering current information into the computer. However, it is more likely that a certain amount of historical data will also be required and this facility will not be available in the normal input routine. For example, a system for recording customers stored the date-of-last-order for each customer. In normal operations this was picked up from the order entry routine. However, on commencement of use of the system, this field was blank in every customer record. This meant that reports running off this field were of little use until the second or third year of the system's use. Consequently a special file creation program has to be written to capture date-of-last-order together with other historical information required by the system.

The designer will have to develop a suite of file creation programs. These will have to be specified, written and tested with the same care as those produced for the proposed operational system. It is likely that a certain amount of re-routing of input data will also be required. For example, the user may be asked for customer details that are then used to create two or three complete or partial files. Validation and verification are vital in file creation programs. It is the stage when the users begin to lose their established filing methods for something that is less tangible. Errors are pounced upon and confidence may quickly ebb away.

The task of organizing the creation of files must also be approached with meticulous detail. Entering 50,000 customer records is a daunting, not to say boring, task. The clerical resources of the department may not be sufficient or willing to undertake such activities on top of their daily work. It may be possible to phase the file creation by entering established records over a period of time, in parallel with the running of the operational system. This requires a certain discipline to ensure that the completion of data entry does not stretch too far into the future and, in addition, it has the disadvantage of the system operating for some considerable time with incomplete files.

In summary, file conversion creates important technical and operational requirements that have to be planned for by the designer. Poor planning may lead to delay or erroneous file creation.

10.4 Preparation of documentation

Documentation is a constant task in systems development. The development methods introduced in this book and its companion text have produced documentation that has been useful in both understanding and communicating the problem area.

However, the latter stages of a project give the opportunity to tidy up this system documentation and to ensure that it actually does reflect the proposed physical system.

Three further types of documentation are associated with the implementation itself.

■ **Training documentation.** This is likely to be concerned with two principal tasks.
  – It will ease the transition from the current system to its successor. Many of the users of the proposed system can better understand its function when it is explained in the context of current procedures.
  – It will provide detailed tuition in the operations of the proposed system. There is a tendency to believe that the functions of the system can be learned from large technical User Manuals. This is very unlikely. Most of the manuals are too long, present all the information at the same level of detail, and describe operations rather than explain them. It is very unlikely that users will have either the time or motivation to work systematically through a large manual. Even if they did, it is uncertain whether they could successfully place the information in the context of their own application and hence separate the important from the trivial. These large manuals fail to recognize the distinction between learning and reference.

Documentation for learning will typically set objectives, explain concepts and commands relevant to those objectives and then test the mastery of these commands to examine whether the objectives have been achieved. Such documentation may use conventional media and methods – handouts, lectures, tests – in the traditional setting of a training course. Alternatively, Computer Based Tuition (CBT) may be considered, particularly where the users are spread geographically and cannot be spared from their everyday tasks. Certainly CBT has particular relevance in computer training as the medium of training is also the objective of that training. The Barclaycard training initiative (Dean and Whitlock, 1983) demonstrates a piggy-backing approach where trainees use identical terminals to those they will use in their everyday work, while a simulation using dummy data permits them to practise precisely the operations that they will carry out in the real system.

- **User documentation.** The point has already been made that user manual should be reference rather than learning documents. Such manuals will need to reflect the expertise and vocabulary of the variety of users involved in the system. It is preferable to write a series of small documents aimed at different types of users rather than one all encompassing tome whose size will ensure that it never gets used. Manuals should concentrate on issues that concern the users most – functions (how to do something) and errors. It is also important to include some information on how to get started.
- **Operations documentation.** The operational details are obviously very important. The system may produce the payslips successfully, but someone must have responsibility for loading the paper at a certain time, readying the printer and collating and distributing the output in accordance with a defined timetable. Operators need training and documentation. They will need to know the normal operating procedures and how to respond to errors.

10.5 Training

Training will cover the retraining of current staff and the recruitment of new personnel. The latter will involve job specifications, advertising, salary advice and interviewing. Retraining will require planning and co-ordination.

For training to be effective, it must be clear what it is trying to achieve. This may be clarified through the setting of objectives. Three levels of objective can be distinguished:

- The first type demands the recall of facts – thus objectives are defined in terms of specific facts that have to be recalled: 'given any department name, the trainee should be able to recall the department code, and vice versa' (Parkin, 1988).
- Comprehension is a different type of objective. In this instance the trainee should be able to 'both recall the facts and describe or illustrate them using words, actions or examples which are different from those the instructor used': 'to be able to give his or her own examples of where a driver should not overtake' Parkin, 1988).

■ Finally, objectives might be defined in terms of application, where the trainee has to use his or her knowledge in different situations of the same general type. Such an objective should not be to appreciate the company's credit rules but: 'Given the customer's time and cash credit limit, and aged balances, decide whether or not to satisfy a request for a stated further amount of credit' (Parkin, 1988).

In practice, the objectives of the training course are likely to be a mixture of recall, comprehension and application.

The setting of objectives for training will suggest ways of delivering that training. The objectives might suggest a combination of media, an approach well demonstrated by the Open University who combine video, audio, tutorial texts, conventional books, case studies, practicals, lectures and CBT in the delivery of their courses.

Once the material has been delivered, the attainment of the trainee and the effectiveness of the training methods can be assessed. The evaluation of the trainee might be through an end of course test, a subjective assessment, a statistical report from the authoring language used to produce the CBT material or some combination of all three. Similarly, the effectiveness of the trainer and the training materials should be assessed (perhaps through an end of course questionnaire) and appropriate action taken.

Unfortunately, too much training is poorly planned and presented at the wrong level, failing to take the expertise and expectations of staff into consideration. To compound this management are often reluctant to give training sessions the time or resources they require. This often manifests itself in the under-funding of training or not releasing staff for sufficient time from their daily duties. As a result many systems are implemented with users and operators who do not fully understand their tasks and roles and this greatly reduces the chance of a successful system.

It should be clear that the tasks of implementation – systems testing, file conversion, documentation and training all require careful planning and co-ordination. Certain tasks must not be left too late (rushed user manuals are usually unimpressive), done too early (operator training months before the system will go live) or in the wrong sequence. Implementation is a project in its own right and will benefit from controls that are applicable to any project. There is sometimes a tendency to relax during implementation believing that all the hard work is done. This is false confidence; lack of control and planning in implementation can undo months of good system and programming work.

10.6 Implementation strategies

The changeover from the old to the new system can be arranged once the computer system is tested and approved. Three possible strategies are available.

10.6.1 Parallel running

In this method the old and new systems are run simultaneously for an agreed period of time and results from the two systems are compared. Once the user has complete confidence in the system the old system is abandoned and transactions are only passed through the new one. Parallel running places a large administrative overhead on the user department because every transaction has to be effectively done twice – once through the established procedures and then again through the new computer system. Results have to be cross-checked and the source of errors located. This will lead to system modifications if problems are discovered in the computer system.

This method does have the advantage of having a 'fail-safe' system to fall back on should the new system crash for some reason. System problems can then be sorted out and the parallel run resumed. However, the duplication of effort can be something of a mixed blessing. Many operators and users still tend to rely on the established system and so some problems never appear until this has been abandoned. In addition, it may be difficult to justify a parallel run for the whole cycle of processing. Problems may only appear at, say, the end of the financial year, months after the 'fail-safe' manual system has been phased out.

10.6.2 Pilot implementation

Two different possibilities exist. The first may be seen as a sort of retrospective parallel running. This takes historical data, say the last 3 months' invoices, and the output produced is compared with the known results. This is only, in effect, a large set of test data, and although this is not a bad thing in itself it does not really give the users and operators the experience and urgency of live processing.

The second type of pilot implementation does use live operations. Instead of all the transactions being passed through the new system, as in parallel running, only a limited number are entered into the computer system. This may be on a sample basis (say 1 in every 10) if this still facilitates cross-checking or, perhaps more realistically, by entering only certain sections, departments or accounts. This gives practice in live processing and reduces the overheads of duplicated entry. It is less rigorous in its testing than parallel running because only a limited set of transactions are used. However, experience suggests that the transaction that causes the system to crash is in the other nine or in another department; a fact that is only found out when the existing system is abandoned and full live running commences.

10.6.3 Direct changeover

The final strategy is to implement the new system completely and withdraw the old without any sort of parallel running at all. Thus processing of the current system may end on a Friday night and all transactions pass through the new computer system from Monday morning onwards. There is no 'fail-safe' system at all. Direct changeover has none of the cost and time overheads of the previous two methods.

Neither does it permit the old loyalty to the replaced system to reflect in the relative performance of the two systems. It clearly demands very thorough testing and well planned file creation and training strategies. All operations of the system must be understood at the moment of going live because the opportunity for gradual training and further testing does not exist. Thus direct changeover is the quickest and most complete of our three implementation strategies but it is probably the riskiest.

In certain instances there is no real alternative to this method. This tends to be:

- Where there is little similarity between the old and the replacement system so that cross checking is not possible.
- Where the cost of parallel running is so prohibitive that it is cheaper to pay for the mistakes of a direct changeover.

Where possible, direct changeovers should occur in slack periods and take advantage of natural breaks in the operations of the organization, such as industrial holidays.

10.7 Post-implementation review

The final delivery of a system provides the opportunity to review the whole conduct of the project. Achievements, failures, surprises and assessments all provide experience that can be used to improve the development of future projects. Thus the review is not only concerned with user satisfaction (and tuning the system to improve that satisfaction), but also with the way that the whole project was conducted. The *quality* of the delivered system and its documentation and training can be monitored through:

- Failure rates;
- Calls to the HELP desk;
- Change requests and the time taken to implement them;
- Statistics concerning the use of the system;
- User satisfaction surveys.

For software houses quality can also be discerned through:

- Profitability;
- Customers returning for further contracts;
- References.

10.8 Conclusion

This chapter has considered the final stages of systems development. It has recognized the significance of testing and the need to approach it in a systematic way. It must also be reiterated that the best method of preventing errors is not to introduce them in the first place. The models introduced in this book and in the companion text have aimed at reducing the chance of error in specification. Research has consistently demonstrated that it is cheaper to fix errors in the early stages of development rather than in the later ones. Both books in this series have tried to lay the foundations of good design.

File conversion, documentation and training all demand attention to detail and an appropriate implementation strategy should be selected and meticulously planned.

Finally, metrics should be established and collected about the quality of the implemented system. Fail errors should be distinguished between code failures, data errors and operational mistakes because each has a different cause and remedy. The calls to the HELP desk must be logged and evaluated. Simple changes in interface, documentation or training might be suggested. The number of functional changes should be logged. Such changes are to be expected because businesses and users change over time. However, we need to log how quickly our design can be modified to take into account these changes. If doubts still linger over whether it was a change or not in the first place ('it's not what I told them I wanted') then specification and sign-off procedures must be reviewed. It is important that improvements are fed back into the development process. Statistical evidence is required to show that our models, prototypes and methods improve system quality. If we leave it as an 'act of faith' then we have little chance of converting the sceptics.

11 Systems Development

11.1 Introduction

In this final chapter we review the objectives and (to a lesser extent) the constraints of design and show that we have not just been concerned with producing abstract models. The techniques really do help achieve our required objectives. The book concludes with a re-statement of the philosophy of the two texts.

11.2 Objectives of design: reviewed

- **Functional**. The system must successfully support the user's requirements. The detail of the design models, particularly for process specification, should mean that we have minimized the chance of misunderstanding requirements. The Logical Data Structure (LDS) is also very precise. It is particularly good at showing what is not supported. The absence of a relationship shows that there is no business connection between these entities. Textual specification of what the system *does not* contain is notoriously weak. Rapid Application Development may have also been used to help the users frame their requirements and indeed prototypes may have been constructed throughout the project.

  In our own company we use the detailed specification as our contract with the user. If our system fails to perform to specification then we have not fulfilled the contract. The contractual nature of the specification should not be underestimated.

- **Efficient**. This is concerned with meeting the functional requirements within the agreed response time. This is primarily achieved through physical design, flexing the logical design to meet required response and processing times. Strategies for flexing were introduced in chapter 8.

  Efficiency should also be extended to effective use of staff resources. For many organizations the cost of Information Systems (IS) staff is the most significant portion of their IS spend. These employees must be used effectively. This means that staff must be clear about what they do and how they do it. The models in this book should form the basis of efficient systems development. Standardized systems development using documented standard products makes it relatively easy for new employees to become productive quickly and for experienced staff to move easily between projects.

The re-usability of code and features is also promoted by object-oriented development and, to a lesser degree, by the modular approach. The increased use of generic models should prevent 'wheel re-invention' and CASE at all levels must increase productivity.

- **Flexible.** Organizations are dynamic. They are affected by internal growth and politics, staff resignations and appointments, administrative reviews and re-organizations, external take-overs, policies and pressures, variations in customer preference and behaviour, economic recessions and political dogma. Consequently, information systems must be easy to adapt to new and changing requirements. Our normalized data design is very flexible. Our process design, if we adopt the top-down approach, less so. Object-oriented development attempts to produce a design that is less process bound. Procedures and precedence can be changed without considerable process re-structuring.

- **Portable.** Portability is closely linked to independence. The rate of technological change means that investment in existing systems will only be preserved if the designer takes effective measures to ensure that little conversion work is required to transfer a system from one computing environment to another. Systems built in this way can harness technical advances rather than reject them on the grounds of the 'cost of the re-write'.

  Our design has been expressed in logical models. The physical implementation has been a relatively late stage in the development lifecycle. Consequently we have a design that has not taken into account temporary physical features and constraints. We also have two design models – one expressing the logical design and the other the physical. A map links the two. If we decide to re-write the system in a new programming language we can work from the logical model (developing a new map in the process) rather than trying to deconstruct the old physical file and program structures.

- **Secure.** Data is a costly and hence valuable resource and so any system that collects and processes it must be resistant to breaches of privacy and confidentiality. Systems must also be designed to meet legislative requirements imposed by the Data Protection Act and the Computer Misuse Act. Chapter 9 has addressed these issues. The Data Dictionary is an important repository of information about acceptable values, formats and business rules.

- **Reliable.** Integrity is a further feature of good design. Parkin describes good integrity when 'all the desired data is accurately recorded, without omission, and stored on the computer safely, so that it is not accidentally or deliberately corrupted or lost'. Thus a system must be trustworthy and accurate and it must be able to demonstrate these qualities to internal and external auditors who have responsibility for checking the validity of the system. The accurate design of inputs and outputs (chapter 2) is important here. The old acronym GIGO (Garbage In–Garbage Out) still applies. Data validation and integrity is an important issues in systems design.

■ **Economical**. The need for a design that demands minimum storage for data and programs is probably a feature that has become less important as hardware costs have declined. Nevertheless, minimizing the amount of redundant data stored by the system reduces problems associated with amendment, insertion and deletion of data. This has been demonstrated in the chapter on data design (chapter 5). Our normalized design produces a system that should not have redundant duplication of data.

■ **Usable**. Emphasis has recently been placed on the assessment of a design by the ease with which it may be learned and operated within acceptable levels of human discomfort, tiredness, effort, etc. Chapter 3 has considered usability in some depth.

■ **Maintainable**. The dynamic nature of business means that requirements must inevitably change over time. It must be easy to make these changes and the effect of implementing these changes must be understood. Good designs are simple and modular, so that the effect of change is both minimized and predictable. Maintenance is also made easier by the availability of accurate and complete documentation.

Maintainability is improved by modular and object-oriented design. In general the system has been self-documenting in that the design process has been through documents and models. These have been produced as a by-product of the process not as a grudging after-thought. Level 3 CASE tools take this concept to the limit – the system is produced from the documentation!

11.2.1 Constraints

Most of the constraints described in chapter 1 are not really relaxed by our design method. However, the interacting issues of cost, time and resources is worth exploring. In many cases the cost of a project has to be estimated early in the development life cycle. Unfortunately, little is known about the project at this point. Consequently 'estimating' is often inspired (or uninspired) guesswork. Manager's find it hard to justify these estimates and under duress of bullying reduce estimates down to what users and clients wish to hear and then subject themselves (and their staff) to unachievable deadlines. DeMarco (1982) summarizes this neatly:

> Some managers don't want good estimators. They want sheep. They want to take cost forecasts directly from the Wishful Thinking Department and force them upon the hapless builders. They expect the builders (under duress of bullying) to regurgitate these numbers and then strive valiantly to meet them.

Within ADAPT we have documented standard tools and techniques including many of those described in this book. At the start of each project a set of tools is selected from the tool-kit and assembled into a project plan. During the project time is recorded against these deliverables. This allows us to compare our predicted cost (and profit margin) with actual costs. It also builds up data about deliverables and permits the construction of standard estimates for these products. Analysis of these figures has allowed us to build an estimating model that can be used to size a system from a few standard variables. This would not have been possible without a disciplined and standard approach to systems development.

This standard approach also makes it easier for companies to gain quality marks such as BS5750 or ISO9001, because they can document and demonstrate that software is constructed using standard procedures.

11.3 Review of methodology

Peter Checkland's (1981) need to attach an appropriate designation to his 'soft systems' work causes him to reflect upon the meaning of such terms as methodology, technique and philosophy. He identifies three conceptions of methodology of which the praxiological 'the science of ... ways of expert procedures' is the one most appropriate to methodologies offered in the commercial systems development marketplace. These methodologies are essentially offering an expert way of doing things.

This book has not adopted a proprietary methodology for four main reasons:

■ None of the methodologies is demonstrably applicable in all development environments. They tend to be more relevant to large organizations with significant computer resources undertaking complex projects. Research has shown that smaller organizations face significant system development problems that need tackling in a systematic way.

Most methodologies tend to over-technicalize development by presenting it as a series of increasingly complex models where the skill of manipulating the model can over-shadow the real-life business application. Kimmerly (1984) accuses many developers of restricted vision. He recognizes the:

> failure of both practising systems analysts and computer science academicians to stress adequately the importance of aesthetics, imagery and other precursors of creativity in the methodology of the discipline.
>
> Due in part to the legacy of various structured revolutions creativity has not only been comprehensively de-emphasized, but has come to be regarded as something to be avoided altogether.

Interestingly, some object-oriented writers (Booch in particular) emphasize the creativity of development.

■ Most methodologies do not appear to significantly recognize the 'organizational context' of the application, or indeed the personal skills of the individual developer.
■ The absence of acceptable metrics and a seeming reluctance to undertake empirical research means that there is little quantitative evidence to support efficiency claims. Journals carry many articles describing different analysis and design techniques but are less blessed with papers about their quantifiable, or even subjective, success.

Consequently the wholesale adoption of a proprietary methodology is not appropriate for general introductory analysis and design training. Proprietary courses are essentially a 'second step' after the developer has mastered basic skills and techniques and is in a better position to appreciate and evaluate the presented methodology.

Hence, the approach of this book has been to select techniques from certain proprietary methodologies where they suit the purpose at hand. A technique (again borrowing from Checkland, 1981) is a specific programme of action that can be practised and learned, and repeatedly executed with a fair chance of success. Some of the techniques we have introduced (such as Relational Data Analysis) are more precise (in learning context) than others (such as Data Flow Diagrams) but we should expect this. Some techniques (such as serving a fast swerving tennis ball) defy repeated success, while others always guarantee the correct result.

The technique approach can be used as:

- A grounding in techniques before examining their detailed use in the context of a proprietary methodology.
- A basis for a 'toolkit' approach to analysis and design that gives the practitioner a set of tools that can be selected to suit different circumstances. This is not dissimilar to the craftsman choosing appropriate tools to undertake different tasks and circumstances.

The toolkit approach seeks to recognize the variety and richness of all real-world applications. This variety manifests itself along three related axes (see figure 11.1):

- Technical. This concerns itself with the technical skills of the developer and with his or her technological knowledge. The mastery of techniques lies along this axis. So do other learning and training skills (network management, COBOL programming, hardware maintenance).
- Organizational. The technical solution will be affected (at least) by the size and structure of the organization, its products, services and geographical distribution, the personalities and skills of the managers concerned and the organizational norms of status, control and reward. Deciding the appropriate technology is not an easy matter. There are plenty of examples where information systems failure has been caused by the selection of a too complex solution, and still others where lack of ambition has led to the under-use of technology. The analyst must be sensitive to the organizational context of his work, understanding that different skills and solutions will be required in what may, at first technical sight, appear to be familiar territory. The great variety of organizational contexts makes us nervous about recommending a 'one best way' approach.
- Human. People model reality in a number of ways. It seems clear that individuals find certain techniques more appealing and comfortable to use. They come to perfectly acceptable solutions by concentrating upon a particular perspective. This is probably most marked in the distinction between the static (entity relationship model) and dynamic (data flow model) of the organization. Some practitioners are more at home with the former and use it to drive their analysis work, while others prefer to concentrate upon the latter. What we must avoid is dogma, typified in a recent prescription by a practitioner that 'entity modelling must come first'. The answer to this is that it depends, both upon the modelling

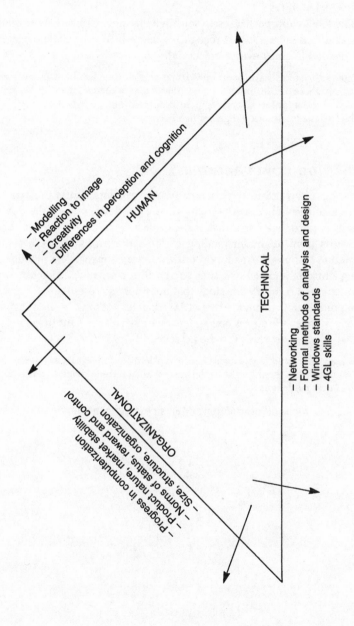

Figure 11.1 Axes of Variety.

perception of the analyst and on the organizational application. Analysts should exclude techniques from their toolkit (after all, they never know when they will need them), but they should recognize and exploit their own modelling preferences and abilities.

The toolkit approach stresses sensitivity to the organization and human issues that confront an analyst. It recognizes that a heavy methodological hammer is not needed to crack every project nut:

> Of course, systems have been built using single strategies or even no formal one. ... However, there are several arguments that strongly suggest that the quality of applications and the application development process is highest when methods representing several strategies are used together in a balanced way.
>
> (Zimmerman, 1983)

11.3.1 Top-down approach

In general, a 'top-down' approach to system development is preferred. This is a reflection of the belief that systems should be developed in the context of the business requirements and that this can best be achieved by building systems downwards from an understanding of the enterprise's strategic requirements. Information systems must support critical business areas. The practice of computerizing 'obvious' applications, such as payroll and accounting ledgers has often led to a fragmented computer strategy that does not use resources effectively.

The point is put succinctly by Ian Macdonald (1988) when he suggests that the key concept of the future is concentrating on what you want to have done, rather than the detail of how this it to be achieved:

> This is a vitally important feature because it places all of the stress in systems development on being able to describe what the business is about. Methodologies must therefore focus on business modelling.

This business focus of information systems development should never be forgotten.

Appendix A
InfoSys Case Study

Introduction

InfoSys is a large multinational company offering information system consultancy, training, publications and software. It currently employs 3,000 employees in 12 countries.

InfoSys runs a small in-house PC training operation for its consultants, lecturers and administrative staff. The operation runs on a 3-monthly cycle. *Nominations* are collected from the Regional Managers and these are used as a basis for creating a course schedule for the next period. A *Nomination List* is sent to the National Manager one month before the next cycle begins together with the course schedule and the course descriptions.

The National Manager's office submit *Course Bookings*, which may or may not be for nominated employees – staff members can go directly to the National Manager if they feel they need a course urgently. These bookings are for particular runs (Course Run) of a particular course (Course Type).

Three days before the course a *Delegate List* is raised and sent to the Lecturer, while *Joining Instructions* are faxed to the Delegate. The lecturer has to complete the Delegate List with an attendance indicator. Non-attendance is an issue and the manager of the section wishes to highlight this in a *Course Performance Report*.

Cancellation and booking changes can be made prior to course commencement and these are recorded. This is also an area that needs monitoring and consequently the manager has asked for a bi-monthly *Change Report*.

Volume Information
Course Types:	15
Course Runs:	30/quarter
Nominations:	150/quarter
Delegates:	180/quarter
Cancellations:	5/quarter
Booking changes:	20/quarter
Average duration of course:	2 days
Lecturers:	2

An analyst has produced a draft Data Flow Diagram and Data Dictionary entries for processes and selected data flows.

Case study

Preview of report
Project: C:\TRIAL\
Title: Systemsdesign
Date: 6-Feb-95 Time: 11:47
Please note that filters were ON for this report generation.
Report: Item details (brief)
This report contains an alphabetic list of all dictionary items and
any details which have been filled in.
Name: Cancel / Rearrange Booking
Type: Process
Notes: Cancellation of Course Bookings are recorded on the Delegate
    details. The Nomination record is also updated so that it will
    re-appear on the next allocation list sent to the National
    Manager. Re-arranged bookings are also noted on the original.
    Delegate entry and a new Delegate entry is created for the
    new arrangements. Data entry checks against Course Run are made
    for this new Delegate occurrence.
Name: Create Nomination
Type: Process
Notes: Nomination Lists are raised quarterly by Regional Managers.
    Data entry checks are made for a valid Course Type and
    Employee. A Nomination occurrence is created.
Name: Create Nomination List
Type: Process
Notes: At the end of each quarter the course registrar sends a list
    of nominations to the National Manager giving proposed courses
    for the next three months and a complete list of nominees (all
    departments) for those courses. The proposed course schedule
    is produced on a spreadsheet and is not included in the scope
    of this application. Nominations close on March 1st for the
    course schedule starting on April 1st. Nominations are to stay
    on the system until their training need is fulfilled OR they
    leave the company OR one year passes since the training was
    requested.
Name: Raise Course Booking
Type: Process
Notes: The National Manager prioritizes training needs and sends in
    Course Bookings. Bookings can be made at any time up to 5 days
    before the scheduled course date. Some bookings are for
    nominated employees, others are not. Entry checks are to be
    made against Course Run and Employee. If the booking is for
    a nominated employee then this has to be indicated in some
    way to ensure that this employee is not included again (for
    that course) in the next allocation list sent to the National
    Manager. A Delegate occurrence is created for each booking.
Name: Raise Delegate List
Type: Process
Notes: Three days before the course is scheduled to run, a delegate
    list is sent to the lecturer and Joining Instructions to the
    Staff Member attending. The Joining Instructions give the
    venue, time and other information. The date the Joining
    Instructions are sent is to be recorded on the Delegate store.
Name: Record Attendance
Type: Process
Notes: The Delegate List is marked by the lecturer to show attendance.
    This course completion is recorded against both Delegate and
    Nomination details.
—-End of Report—-

Data dictionary entries: data flows

Data flow name: nominations
From: Regional Manager   To: Raise Nomination

Region no:	Region description	Nominated by:		
01	North	Stan Cummings		
Course code	**Course description**	**Staff-id**	**Staff name**	
W101	WORD Introduction	E12657	C. Tildesley	
W101	WORD Introduction	E32451	T. Thomas	
W102	WORD Advanced	E31562	J. Smith	
W102	WORD Advanced	E12657	C. Tildesley	
W102	EXCEL Introduction	E45611	J. Farmer	

Data flow name: nomination list
From: Raise Nomination List   To: National Manager

Course code	Course description	Staff-id	Staff name	region
W101	WORD Introduction	E12657	C. Tildesley	North
W101	WORD Introduction	E32451	T. Thomas	North
W101	WORD Introduction	E54678	H. Harris	South
W101	WORD Introduction	E98462	T. Jones	South
W101	WORD Introduction	E75612	J. Smith	West
W101	WORD Introduction	E55661	F. Reeder	West
W102	WORD Advanced	E31562	J. Smith	North
W102	WORD Advanced	E12657	C. Tildesley	North
W102	WORD Advanced	E54678	H. Harris	South
W102	WORD Advanced	E66778	B. Bugle	East

Data flow name: course booking
From: National Manager   To: Raise Course Booking

Region no:	Region description	Nominated by:		
01	North	Stan Cummings		
Run code	**Course date**	**Course code**	**Staff-id**	**Staff name**
0001	05/01/95	W101	E09753	A. Bishop
0001	05/01/95	W101	E12657	C. Tildesley
0002	12/01/95	W102	E54642	A. Fisher
0006	14/02/95	W101	E54642	C. Hoyles
0012	15/03/95	E101	E33342	L. Tripp
0012	15/03/95	E101	E31562	J. Smith

```
Data flow name: delegate list
From: National Manager                 To: Lecturer
```

Run code:	0012
Course type:	E101
Venue:	Room 102, InfoSys House
Course name:	Introduction to Excel
Lecturer name:	Graham Martin
Duration:	2 days
Start date:	15/03/95

Staff-id	Staff name/Region	Joining instructions sent	Attended
E33342	L. Tripp: North	12/03/93	
E31562	J. Smith: North	12/03/93	
E44339	W. Nolan: West	13/03/93	
E11557	A. Ridout: East	13/03/93	

Note: Lecturer must complete Attended column and return (Data Flow: Course Attendance Sheet)

Two further report are required. These are not shown on the Data Flow Diagram

Course performance report
January 1995

Run code	Course date	Course code	Venue	Staff-id	Staff name	Attended
0001	05/01/95	W101	Room 102	E09753	A. Bishop	Y
				E12657	C. Tildesley	Y
				E66311	T. Smith	Y
				E67322	H. Blundell	N

Attended: 3 Did Not Attend: 1

0002	12/01/95	W102	Room 105	E54642	A. Fisher	Y
				E55097	T. Austin	N

Attended: 1 Did Not Attend: 1

0003	12/01/95	E101	Room 102	E55997	F. Reinhard	N
				E66422	T. Cliff	Y
				E77322	J. Jones	N

Attended: 1 Did Not Attend: 2

Change report for period 01/01/95 to 01/03/95

Staff-id	Run code	Booked date	Change date	Change reason	Comments
E87654	0002	11/12/94	21/12/94	Cancel	Left company
E11342	0002	14/12/94	10/01/95	Change	No reason
E21109	0003	03/01/85	11/01/95	Change	No reason
E98231	0004	04/01/95	09/01/95	Cancel	No reason
E13983	0011	12/01/95	14/02/95	Change	Meeting clash
E17652	0013	13/02/95	17/02/95	Cancel	Mis-booking
E32178	0020	17/02/95	23/02/95	Change	No reason

Appendix B
Further Reading

Chapter 1

Coad P. and Yourdon E. *Object-oriented Analysis*, 2nd edn, Yourdon Press, 1991

Parkinson J. *Making CASE work* NCC Blackwell, 1991

Schott F. and Olson M. Designing Usability in Systems:Driving for Normalcy, *Datamation*, 15 May 1988, pp 68–76

Shackel B. Ergonomics in the Design for Usability, *Proceedings of the Second Conference of the British Computer Society Human Computer Interaction Specialist Group*, 23–26 September 1986, pp 44–64

Skidmore S. *Introducing Systems Analysis* NCC Blackwell, 1994

Slusky L. Integrating Software Modelling and Prototyping Tools, *Information and Software Technology*, September 1987, vol 29, no 7

Windsor J. Are Automated Tools Changing Systems Analysis and Design?, *Journal of Systems Management*, November 1986

Yourdon E. Whatever Happened to Structured Analysis, *Datamation*, 1 June 1986, pp 133–138

Chapters 2 and 3

Abbott J. *Presentation of Computer I/O for People* NCC Publications, 1983

Adie C. *SAA and the Common User Access*, EXE, July 1988, pp 10–15

Coats R. and Vlaeminke I. *Man-Computer Interfaces, a Guide for Software Design and Implementation* Blackwell, 1988

Din A. *Structured Query Language* NCC Blackwell, 1994

Mehlmann M. *When People Use Computers – an Approach to Developing an Interface* Prentice-Hall, 1981

Microsoft, *The Windows Interface – an Application Design Guide* Microsoft, 1992

Parfett M. *What is EDI?*, 2nd edn, NCC Blackwell, 1992

Schott F. and Olson M. Designing Usability in Systems:Driving for Normalcy, *Datamation*, 15 May 1988, pp 68–76.

Skidmore S. Farmer R. and Mills G. *SSADM Version 4: Models and Methods*, 2nd edn, NCC Blackwell, 1995

Chapter 4

Alavi M. An Assessment of the Prototyping Approach to Information Systems Development, *Communications of the ACM*, June 1984, vol. 27, no. 6

Basili V. and Turner A. Iterative Enhancement: a Practical Technique for Software Development, *IEEE Tutorial: Structured Programming*, No7CH1049–6, September 1975

Belbin P.M. *Management Teams* Heinemann, 1981

Booch G. *Object-oriented Analysis and Design*, 2nd edn, Benjamin/Cummings, 1994

Boehm B. Prototyping versus Specifying: a Multi-project Experiment, *IEEE Transactions on Software Engineering*, vol. SE 10, no. 3, May 1984

Costello J. Radical Ways to Help Projects, *Computer Weekly*, 20/06/91

Dearnley P. and Mayhew P. In Favour of System Prototypes and Their Integration into the Systems Development Cycle, *The Computer Journal*, vol. 26 no. 1, 1983

Gremillion L. and Pyburn P. Breaking the systems Development Bottleneck, *Harvard Business Review*, 1983, (01C2), p.133

Lantz K. *The Prototyping Methodology* Prentice-Hall, 1984

Martin J. *Fourth Generation Languages*, vols 1 and 2, Savant Research Institute, 1984

Merlyn V. Is RAD 'RAD'?, *Software Magazine*, 08/02/91

Naumann J.D. and Jenkins A.M. Prototyping: The new paradigm for Systems Development, *MIS Quarterly*, September 1982

Tudor D. and Tudor I. *Systems Analysis and Design – a Comparison of Structured Methods* NCC Blackwell, 1994

Chapter 5

Benyon D. *Information and Data Modelling* Blackwell Scientific, 1990

Codd E.F. A Relational Model of Large Shared Data Banks, *Communications of the ACM*, vol.13, no. 6, June 1970, pp 377–387

Codd E.F. Further Normalisation of the Data Base Relational Model, *Current Computer Science Symposium 6: Data Base Systems*, Prentice-Hall, May 1971, pp 65–98

Date C. *An Introduction to Database Systems*, vol. 1, 5th edn, Addison-Wesley, 1991

Howe D. *Data Analysis for Data Base Design*, 2nd edn, Edward Arnold, 1989

Kent W. A Simple Guide to Five Normal Forms in Database Theory, *Communications of the ACM*, vol 26, no 2, May 1983, pp 120–125

Chapter 6

Coleman M. and Pratt S. *Software Engineering* Chartwell-Bratt, 1986

Gilbert P. *Software Design and Development* SRA, 1983

Page-Jones M. *Practical Guide to Structured Systems Design*, 2nd edn, Prentice-Hall, 1988

Skidmore S. Farmer R. and Mills G. *SSADM Version 4: Models and Methods*, 2nd edn, NCC Blackwell, 1995

Chapter 7

Booch G. *Object-oriented Analysis and Design*, 2nd edn, Benjamin/Cummings, 1994

Coad P. and Yourdon E. *Object-oriented Design* Yourdon Press, 1991

Coad P. and Yourdon E. *Object-oriented Analysis*, 2nd edn, Yourdon Press, 1991

Cook S. Daniels J. *Designing Object Systems* Prentice-Hall, 1994
Graham I. *Object Oriented Methods,* 2nd edn, Adddison-Wesley, 1994
Martin J. and Odell J. *Object-oriented Analysis and Design* Prentice-Hall, 1992
Meyer B. *Object-oriented Software Construction* Prentice-Hall, 1988
Rumbaugh J. *et al. Object-oriented Modelling and Design* Prentice-Hall, 1991
Shlaer A. and Mellor S. *Object-oriented Systems Analysis* Yourdon Press, 1988
Ward P. Mellor S. *Structured Development for Real-Time Systems* Yourdon Press, 1985

Chapter 8

Atre S. *Database: Structured Techniques for Design, Performance and Management* Wiley, 1980
Booch G. *Object-oriented Analysis and Design,* 2nd edn, Benjamin/Cummings, 1994
Bradley J. *File and Data Base Techniques,* Holt-Saunders, 1982
Page-Jones M. *Practical Guide to Structured Systems Design,* 2nd edn, Prentice-Hall, 1988
Pratt P. and Joseph R. *Database Systems: Management and Design* Boyd and Fraser, 1987
Rumbaugh J. *et al. Object-oriented Modelling and Design* Prentice-Hall, 1991
Weiderhold G., *Database Design,* McGraw-Hill, 1983

Chapter 9

Bhaskar *et al. Computer Security: Threats and Countermeasures* NCC Blackwell, 1993
Chambers A. *Computer Auditing* Pitman, 1986
Elbra T. *Guide to the Data Protection Act* NCC Publications, 1984
Elbra T. *A Practical Guide to the Computer Misuse Act,* NCC Blackwell, 1990
Elbra T. *Computer Security Handbook,* NCC Blackwell, 1992
Martin J. *Security, Accuracy and Privacy in Computer Systems* Prentice-Hall, 1973
Norman A. *Computer Insecurity,* Chapman and Hall, 1983
Warner M. and Stone M. *The Data Bank Society* Allen and Unwin, 1970
Wong K. *Computer Security: Risk Analysis and Control* NCC Publications, 1977

Chapter 10

Dean C. and Whitlock D. *Computer Based Training* Kogan-Page,1983
Keen J. *Managing Systems Development* Wiley,1981
Parkin A. *Systems Analysis,* 2nd edn, Edward Arnold, 1988

Chapter 11

Checkland P. *Systems Thinking, Systems Practice* Wiley 1981
de Marco T. *Controlling Software Projects* Yourdon Press, 1982
Kimmerly W. Restricted Vision, *Datamation,* 1984, pp 152–160
Macdonald I. Automating Information Engineering, in Benyon D. and Skidmore S. (eds) *Automating Systems Development* Plenum Press, 1988
Zimmerman R. Phases, Methods and Tools - a triad of systems development, in Davis *et al.* (eds) *Entity-Relationship Approach to Software Engineering* Elsevier, 1983

Appendix C
Exercises

Chapter 1
Case study

1. Walkthrough the InfoSys documentation provided in Appendix A.

The analyst who produced this documentation is leaving tomorrow for a new job in America. He has agreed to a meeting with you in the morning to examine any issues you need clarifying. Make a list of any points you would wish to clarify at that meeting.

The following question does not apply to the case study.
2. Assess a representative CASE tool against the features listed by Slusky. Determine whether it is a CASE 1, 2 or 3 tool or something in-between (or more!)

Chapter 2
Case study questions

1. Design suitable documents for the:

- Nomination Form;
- Course Booking Form.

You can assume, for the moment, that InfoSys intend to enter data via keyboard transcription of manually prepared documents.

2. Design a suitable layout for the
- Course Performance Report;
- Delegate List.

3. One of the directors at InfoSys is interested in direct data entry. Re-draft the Course Booking Form designed in exercise 1 to make it appropriate to OMR entry. Discuss the reasons for the changes you have incorporated. Would OMR be appropriate for this application?

The following question does not apply to the case study.
4. Visit three shops offering Charge Cards and collect an application form for the card. Compare the three cards on the following aspects, highlighting examples of good and bad design:

- Order of questions;
- Number of questions;
- Wording of questions;
- Consistency within the form;
- Clarity and Language of supplementary notes;
- Use of colour;
- Use of shading;
- Use of space and spacing;
- Ease of keyboard data entry;
- Appropriate questions. Are there any questions you find unacceptable?

Chapter 3
Case study questions

1. Produce an input screen design appropriate for the entry of the data on the forms you designed in the previous chapter:

- Nomination Form;
- Course Booking Form.

2. For the entry of the Course Booking Form, develop a:

- Logical Dialogue Outline;
- Input/Output Structure Chart;
- State Transition Diagram.

Assess each of these models for:

- Ease of interpretation by the end user;
- Ease of construction;
- Ease of modification;
- Usefulness to the programmer;
- Error handling in the dialogue.

The following question does not apply to the case study.

3. Package selection is often unduly affected by the interface of the product. Examine two competing software packages and assess their interface against the criteria for an effective interface outlined in section 3.1. The competing products can be application software (such as integrated accounts), general software (e.g. spreadsheets or DBMS products), CASE tools or even Operating Systems. The comparison may also suggest other factors that should be taken into account when producing an effective interface. List these down as well and justify their inclusion in the assessment criteria.

Chapter 4
Case study

1. InfoSys is considering developing the system in three prototypes. The first will be ready in 10 days time, the second in 1 month and the third in 3 months time.

Given these deadlines, what would you suggest might be the content and purpose of each prototype?

2. One of the proposed users of the InfoSys system is particularly concerned about the entry of course bookings

Construct, using an appropriate method and tools, a prototype for this area. You must:

- State whether the prototype is a 'full' (build-on) or 'mock-up' (throw-away) product;
- Provide a form to allow the user to comment on the prototype;
- Document the time spent on prototype construction.

The following question does not apply to the case study.
3. Examine the prototyping features of two competing Fourth Generation Languages. Further assess the scope of the 4GL by examining its features against the checklist given in section 4.3 of the text. Are there other facilities you might wish to include in this checklist? List these down as well and justify their inclusion in the assessment.

Chapter 5
Case study

1. Produce normalization working papers for the following:

- Nomination Form;
- Course Booking Form;
- Course Performance Report;
- Delegate List;
- Course Nomination List;
- Change Report.

2. Develop a consolidated relation list from the working papers listed above.
3. Construct a Logical Data Model (with optionality and naming conventions added) for the consolidated list given in exercise 2. List any assumptions you have made.

The following question does not apply to the case study.
4. Investigate Fourth and Fifth Normal Forms and provide examples. How will these Forms 'appear' in our step by step procedural approach and does our method help identify and capture either or both of them?

Chapter 6

1. Write Action Diagrams for the following processes:

- Create nomination;
- Create course booking;
- Record cancellations and transfers.

2. Construct an Entity/Event grid for the InfoSys application.
3. For each entity construct an Entity Life History showing operations and State Indicators.
4. Construct an Update Process Model for the events:

- Receipt of a nomination;
- Receipt of course booking.

5. Compare the Update Process Model with the Action Diagrams developed in exercise 1.
6. Develop a Logical Access Map for the processes:

- Produce Course Nomination List;
- Raise Course Performance Report;
- Produce Change Report.

The following question does not apply to the case study.

7. Review the Structure Chart notation described in Page-Jones (1988). Try and apply it to the simple order processing example developed in this chapter (make and list any assumptions). How does it fare against the assessment criteria suggested in section 6.7?

Chapter 7

1. Construct an object state model for InfoSys and compare it with the Logical Data Model developed in exercise 5.3.
2. Model object behaviour by using a standardized textual specification within each object.
3. Produce a State chart for the object Employee (or your equivalent).
4. InfoSys management are keen to introduce standardized joining instructions (JI) into the system.

The JI is a letter mainly constructed from standard paragraphs. It is agreed that:

- Part of the JI will consist of text about a specific location, e.g. hotel, its location, map of how to get there, dress requirements, etc.
- Another part of the JI will be about the specific type of course. These are always of the same duration and may have special requirements (bring along extra folder, pre-course reading, etc.).
- Another part of the JI will be about the particular run of the course; precise time and date of start and finish, together with any particular features of that run such as the lecturer, special attendance by manager, etc.
- Finally, the JI will be sent to the prospective delegate and the date of despatch noted somewhere in the system.

Produce a draft object model for this extension to the system requirements. Why might a Logical Data Model be less appropriate to this application. Make and state assumptions.

The following question does not apply to the case study.

5. Investigate the Z notation and assess its potential use in object-oriented development and its performance against the criteria established in section 6.7 of the text. A starting point might be Wordsworth *Software Development with Z*, Addison-Wesley, 1992.

Chapter 8

1. Implement the InfoSys system using appropriate software and document the differences between the logical and the physical data design.
2. Produce a map showing the connection between process logic and program implementation. Discuss the usefulness of the logical model(s) against the criteria summarized in section 8.8.

The following question does not apply to the case study.

3. Investigate Object-oriented DBMS and summarize the state of the art.

Chapter 9

1. Specify an audit trail for the InfoSys system.
2. Discuss the implications of the Data Protection Act and the Computer Misuse Act to the InfoSys application.
3. Assess how well the following techniques model the control requirements of the system:

- Data Flow Diagram;
- Logical Data Model;
- Input/Output Structure Diagram;
- Logical Dialogue Outline;
- Action Diagram;
- Update Process Model;
- State chart.

The following question does not apply to the case study.

4. Investigate the current state of the Data Protection Act. Have recent guidelines been issued? New exemptions created? Case law established? Prosecutions made? Penalties imposed? Is there any dispute between the Registrar and credit assessment agencies?

Chapter 10
Case study

1. Develop a plan for the testing of the InfoSys system.
2. List the documentation that will be provided with the proposed system.
3. Draw up training objectives and schedule, together with recommendations about how training might be delivered.
4. What implementation strategy will be used and why?

The following question does not apply to the case study.

5. Investigate the scope, facilities and cost of testing tools and identify the advantages they offer to an organization.

Chapter 11
Case study

1. Review and assess your InfoSys design against the objectives defined in section 11.2 of the text.
2. If we are to construct a tool-kit approach to systems development then we must record where we found particular things to be useful and where we did not. In the context of the case study list the tools and techniques introduced in this book and write a short note for each outlining areas where you think their application would be useful and circumstances where you found them marginal or no use at all.

The following question does not apply to the case study.

3. Investigate and discuss the following

- 'Off-shore' systems development. Systems are specified in one country (say, England) and written elsewhere (India, Malaysia, Russia)
- Facilities management and 'outsourcing'.

What are the implications of the tools and techniques described in this book to such developments (and vice versa)?

Index